CORRECTION

Mistake Management: a positive approach
for language teachers

MARK BARTRAM
RICHARD WALTON

LTP
TEACHER
TRAINING

Language Teaching Publications
114a Church Road, Hove, BN3 2EB, England
email: ltp@ltpwebsite.com

Acknowledgements
The authors would like to thank the following people and
institutions for their help in the preparation of this book:
Jimmie Hill (especially chapter 9)
Michael Lewis
Graham Simpson
Roberta Longo
Fiametta Pignatti
The staff and students of the Cambridge School, Verona; UTS
Oxford Centre, Oxford; Abon Language School, Bristol.

Cover design by Anna Macleod.
Typeset by Blackmore Typesetting Services, Brighton.
Printed in England by Commercial Colour Press, London E7.

EDITOR'S INTRODUCTION

Learning a language is a complicated activity. A lot of research has been done in to how to make learning effective but, as yet, it remains surprisingly difficult to say with certainty what methods are truly more effective than others. There is a lot of theory, and even a lot of evidence, but it remains largely inconclusive.

In addition, however, there remain a great many prejudices. Most people – whether they are language teachers, parents, or language students – have strongly held beliefs about how they should learn and, equally strongly, about how they should not. Unfortunately, many of these beliefs are exactly that – beliefs and not facts. They may be strongly held, but they have no firm basis. One of the subjects upon which most people have strongly held beliefs is the role played by correction.

Many years of working with language teachers – experienced and inexperienced, native speakers and non-native speakers of English, traditional and progressive, employed in State schools and private schools, has shown me that one certain way to rouse a group of language teachers to heated discussion is to question their attiutude to correction. A simple remark such as 'Most language teachers probably correct their students too much' can easily provoke aggression, anger and many other unhelpful attitudes. The fact is, the question of the teacher's attitude to mistakes and correction is probably the single most important issue in a language teacher's professional development. In many ways, it is also central for students. The kind of activities the teacher encourages in the classroom, and the kind which the teacher avoids or minimises, will be strongly influenced by the teacher's views of the role of mistakes and correction in learning.

Many factors need to be taken into account – age, situation, purpose, previous learning experience etc. It is difficult to be dogmatic. But it is surely reasonable to say that the teacher's attitude to correction should be based on mature reflection on certain issues, and accurate observation of what actually happens in his or her own classes. That is precisely what the authors set out to achieve in this book.

As they themselves openly admit in the first pages of the book, the very act of writing the book changed their attitudes to some of these questions. I know that my own attitudes have changed over the years. In general, for myself, it would be true to say that the longer I taught, the less I corrected. That is, I suspect, the general direction of the authors' own thinking.

The purpose of this book, however, is not to impose that attitude on readers. It is, rather, an invitation to think about your own attitudes and your own teaching. The authors provide a long sequence of questions which they invite the reader to consider. While they are not afraid to give their own answers to the questions, they are equally unafraid to admit that there are other attitudes and other possibilities. The book represents very clearly something of the authors' own journey towards a wider and more balanced understanding of the role of correction, and of various practical possibilities for its effective implementation.

Some years ago a teacher in a seminar I was conducting observed 'Of course I have to correct, that's my job'. He placed a heavy stress on the word 'that'. In a world of uncertainties, we can be certain of one thing – that particular teacher had too narrow a view of his own role as a teacher. However successful he was in what he did, there were many things he could have done, which he had not yet discovered. Yet he was probably much more typical than teacher training departments and course tutors would like to think.

Many language teachers see correction as an area where they can be certain in the uncertain world of language teaching. This book invites them to follow an intellectual and personal journey. At first they may find it disconcerting, because the role given to correction is much more ambiguous than some teachers would like. At the same time, the authors provide many opportunities for readers to deepen and widen their understanding of language, of learning, and, equally excitingly, of the teacher's own role. It is this which, for me, makes it worth thinking about the role of correction. Too often a narrow attitude to that issue prevents teachers from a wider and more fulfilling role for themselves, quite apart from providing their students with richer and more rewarding learning experiences.

I believe this book, while in many ways inviting teachers to a more student-centred approach, also promises teachers the prospect of real personal and professional development.

Michael Lewis   Hove, April 1991

iv

CONTENTS

HOW TO USE THIS BOOK

It is possible to read this book from start to finish on your own. You will find new ideas to try out, and some questions to answer about your teaching principles and practice. However, we also believe that an essential part of teacher development is the discussion with other teachers in a similar position to you which a book like this tries to provoke.

In the "task-boxes" which occur regularly throughout the text, we have included exercises for you to do with colleagues. Some of these involve watching colleagues' lessons, and inviting them to watch yours. While we realise that in many schools this can be difficult, we do believe that it can be of great help – not because it allows you to see whether your colleagues are better or worse teachers, but because firstly as an observer it gives you a host of new ideas and insights, and secondly, as an observee, it provides an objective viewpoint without being too judgmental or evaluative.

A second technique which we believe is useful is the tape-recording or video-recording of your lessons. Many teachers describe their lessons in one way (quite honestly) when a more objective view suggests a rather different picture. Sometimes, teachers literally are not aware of what they are doing. Recording tells you what you are really doing.

Note: before you start working through the task boxes, it will be a good idea to record two or three of your lessons. You should tape complete lessons. Make sure you record a good variety of levels (if you can) and a good variety of types of activity. These recordings will be needed for some of the tasks, and will save you having to record a fresh lesson every time you start a new task.

These activities need to be presented and explained to the students. Otherwise, they may tend to believe **they** are being checked or tested. As always, it is vital to communicate with the students.

Finally, the task-boxes often ask you to discuss questions with your colleagues. These boxes could therefore provide the basis for discussions during teacher development sessions in your school or college. But maybe you do not have regular sessions of this kind; perhaps you do not even have colleagues! In these cases you have to go out and look for people to talk to: ask your Director if you can start teacher development sessions in your school; join the local Teachers' Club – if there isn't one, start one; put up advertisements in local schools to see if others are interested. It is rare, even in the smallest places, to be the only teacher interested in personal and professional development.

INTRODUCTION

When we first sat down to write this book, we had two very strong beliefs.

The first was that mistakes – why students make them, and how teachers can deal with them – are of crucial and central importance in teaching languages.

This led to a certain line of thinking: mistakes must be categorised (into 'errors', 'slips', 'lapses', and, of course, 'mistakes'), their causes diagnosed (interference from the mother tongue, hypothesis-making within the target language, Friday afternoon tiredness), and suitable treatments devised (finger techniques, correcting codes, writing workshops). Many of these are certainly of value, and are discussed later in the book.

The second idea was that teachers, on the whole, are a homogeneous group of thinking people who would be grateful for a simple, coherent set of principles about mistakes and their correction by which they could operate on a day-to-day basis.

As time has gone by, however, we have become less and less convinced of these two ideas: or, rather, they have undergone considerable revision in our minds. Firstly, we have become convinced that, to some extent, the whole area of mistakes is one that teachers (and, more importantly, learners) have accepted as an essential part of language teaching and learning. They have persuaded themselves that mistakes and correction are important. That phrase 'to some extent' is the crucial one. We are not saying that mistakes are not important; but perhaps not as much as we thought, or as much as we have been led to think. We believe that 'mistake-obsession' is not generally found outside the world of language teaching and learning. It is teachers and learners who have invented and perpetuated it. Furthermore, we believe that an obsession with mistakes affects learners' general progress adversely.

Secondly, we have found that, despite the generally very high levels of specialised teacher training for language teachers, there is an enormous variety of practice and attitudes to mistakes and particularly mistake-correction. This ranges from teachers who have never given it a single thought – which is not to say they do not correct – to those who worry about it constantly. We also believe that certain groups of teachers – perhaps those who lack confidence in their own English – worry more because they feel they have to make decisions about the rightness/wrongness of their students' English.

This book is for both groups. Its aim is to encourage teachers to think about mistakes and their correction, whilst trying to persuade them that the importance which the topic claims for itself inside the profession is exaggerated. Teachers who see it as unimportant are asked to think more, worried teachers to worry less! In particular, by encouraging teachers to examine and assess their own principles and practice – which we believe are often far apart – we hope to let them take decisions about their own teaching, in the same way that we ask students to take responsibility for their own learning.

David Nunan*, in research done into the decisions made by teachers in the classroom, has found that relatively few of their decisions concern mistakes and mistake-management. Only 4% of all pedagogical decisions are to do with correction and feedback.

In some ways, this conclusion should be surprising to us, since teachers sometimes talk as if they are deciding and thinking all the time about whether to correct or not!

Teacher Development

We define teacher development (TD) as the constant and on-going re-energising of a teacher's technique whilst the teacher is actually in the job. Many teachers come off short, intensive initial training courses and then find a job which may last for three or four years before they ever need to think about the nuts and bolts of their work again. If they are fortunate, they will find in-service training schemes, or teachers' clubs, which help them to build on their initial training, but these can be rare. Usually teachers have to wait until they have saved up enough time and

* David Nunan: "The Teacher as Decision-Maker" – paper presented at IATEFL conference, Exeter, April 1991.

money to go on a longer 'training' course.

While we recognise the value of these training courses, they are not quite the same thing as teacher development: they energise and improve the teacher, but usually only for the period of the course itself. The follow-up to them is often short-lived.

Teacher development, on the other hand, means the constant questioning of both the general principles by which our teaching is guided, and the specific practice which we actually adopt. These two things can be a long way apart. For example, on the issue of teacher talking time: many teachers believe that (a) it is 'bad' technique for the teacher to talk a lot in class and (b) they personally talk very little! TD encourages the teacher to ask: are these beliefs true?

This is not done with the intention only of changing or undermining beliefs and established practices; in many cases, teachers will end up still persuaded of their original position. Its real purpose is to provide a continuing refreshment and critique of what is, and what should be, happening in the classroom.

As far as mistakes are concerned, we are encouraging teachers to ask these questions:

> **Are mistakes important?**
> **Does correcting them really do any good?**
> **Can it do harm?**
> **What do I actually do in class?** (as opposed to what I think I do, or what I think I ought to do)
> **How could I change or improve what I do in class?**

These are the central questions behind this book.

It is very important to stress that the main function of this book is to provoke teachers into asking themselves these and other questions about their teaching: it does not provide the answers, which must come from the teachers themselves. Above all, we hope to show that, as learners must become more and more responsible for their own learning, so teachers must become responsible for their own teaching. In this way, their work will be constantly re-vitalised.

CHAPTER ONE

BACKGROUND THEORY

Some teachers hate theory. If you are one of these, please do not ignore this section! Even if you hate theory, it is not possible to avoid it. It is like politics: you may say 'I hate politics' and not vote, but even abstention is a political point of view. Everything you do in the classroom is based upon a belief that certain kinds of teaching or learning work better than others.

For example, take the simplest of actions by the teacher: saying 'Hello' to the students at the start of a lesson. Do you say it in the native language or in the target language? Do you say it with your normal voice or a special clear 'teacher's' voice? Do you insist your students reply or not? **Why** do you do it in the way you do?

Similarly with mistakes: all students make them, and all teachers react to them. Some react by doing nothing; others react too severely; some explain the mistake elegantly to the class. And all these reactions, consciously or unconsciously, are part of the teacher's theory of language learning, and where mistakes fit into that. In many ways, a teacher can be defined by his or her attitude to mistakes.

The problem is that, too often, that attitude is unconscious. If your friend is stung by a wasp, you may react in a number of ways: do nothing, suck the wound, pour boiling water on it and so on. But generally you have not thought about it in advance, and your reaction may therefore be irrational or clumsy: like many amateur first-aiders, you may end up doing more damage than the original injury. The same is true of correcting mistakes in language learning – often the spontaneous reaction on hearing a mistake is to correct it immediately.

This is why theory, in the end, is important. How you react to a mistake is part of your whole vision of what a language is, what learning is, and what a teacher is. Unless you are exceptional in some way, you would probably agree that thinking through these issues is beneficial to your teaching – and will, eventually, affect it. For this reason, we start with some more general considerations.

1.1 What is language? Why do people learn second languages?

TASK 1

Think about the students in one of your current classes. Rank them in order of their English.
Now make a list of the criteria you used.

Is a language something that you study or something you use? Both, of course. You can study a language and never use it – like Latin. But most people want to use it, either for strictly practical purposes (for example, in order to be allowed to fly a plane) or wider, cultural or educational reasons. Very few students are interested in the language for its own sake. A language is a system of communication, and most students will use it as a practical skill.

The main implication of this is that a good language user is one who manages to communicate well. Comprehensibility is the aim, not perfection. When a person says someone's English is good, because s/he makes very few mistakes, you can be sure that the person making the judgment is a language teacher.

Equally, it is true that, unlike other subjects which you study, there is a wide range of 'correctness' in a language. One would say that in mathematics $3 + 8 = 12$ is wrong; there are no circumstances in which it could be right; it makes no sense to call it 'nearly right'. But what about the second speaker here:

A Have you seen Frank today?

B No, but I've seen him yesterday.

This is obviously 'wrong' structurally – an English person would normally use the past simple. But it communicates the meaning completely successfully. We could call such language 'nearly right'. It is quite different from a sentence such as *Like visit station train in the zoo* which is both 'wrong' and, more importantly, incomprehensible.

Furthermore, we tend to think of the target language as a single, unified body of rules and usages. But this is not true: all languages, and especially English, have a wide variety of forms, regional, national, dialectal, formal/informal, colloquial/careful, old fashioned/modern. Language is also constantly changing, admitting new words and new usages from other languages, and leaving behind old ones which no longer serve a purpose. Any native speaker will be in doubt about certain areas of English. Is there a hyphen in *lamp-post*? How do you spell the *-ing* form of the verb *tie*? Can I say *different to*, or will people object? Even the dictionaries disagree about some things. We are in doubt, and being in doubt is not a problem. In certain circumstances, it is more helpful to say *I don't know* than to insist on providing a 'correct' answer which, in fact, is wrong or incomplete.

It is important to remember, therefore, and especially for non-native-speaker teachers, that anybody's knowledge of a language, including their own, is partial. A teacher must be very careful about saying that a particular form is 'wrong'. It may be wrong in London, but perfectly acceptable in Jamaica. It may be wrong in a speech but perfectly acceptable in a playground. It may be a form that the teacher has never seen, but which in fact exists.

Task 2

The following are all examples of real English, produced by adult native-speakers (in one case, the Prime Minister, another from an EFL textbook).

How do you react to them?

1. The situation is getting more worse every day.
2. Us is the same.
3. This fact bore down more hardly on the working classes than any other.
4. The course will run July 5th through August 5th.
5. If we'd have found a faulty cooker, we would have named it.
6. Less people are unemployed today than a year ago.
7. There's seven of them.
8. Which of these two jokes do you think is best?
9. Christmas Tree's for sale - £5 each.
10. Where's your purse to?

Now turn to page 119 and see if you agree with our comments.

Teachers may find it more useful to think of a 'spectrum of likelihood' – with forms being more or less likely to occur – especially in particular situations or media of expression.

Even native-speakers do not understand the grammar of their own language in its entirety, and certainly do not know all the variations of it. There is no point in 'correcting' a student only to find they learnt their English in Alabama, Nairobi or Sydney! The job of language teachers is to present the language they speak, rather than criticise students for speaking a form of it which is different from theirs. We do not correct our American friends when they say *I didn't see that movie yet*, so why should we correct our Spanish or Japanese friends if they say the same thing?

1.2 What is a teacher?

One role that the teacher has often enacted within a society is that of the upholder of the traditions and values of that society. Teachers often transmit the received social values to succeeding generations. The teacher in this model is a figure of high social status – though rarely high pay – who is regarded as an oracle by students and others. The teacher has knowledge which must be transferred or passed on to the new generation.

The vast, worldwide boom in TEFL has, on the surface, produced a new kind of teacher. Rather than being on a pedestal, s/he is now a 'paid adviser', a kind of linguistic doctor. The student is sometimes older, richer and more worldly than the teacher. However, teachers can still maintain a superior position because they know the language.

This superiority is manifested through the mistake: the student says something wrong, the teacher finds the mistake, and corrects it – in the same way as a patient feels ill, the doctor diagnoses it, and then operates. The relationship is still essentially a superior/inferior one.

> ## TASK 3
>
> Do you ever use mistake-correction as a weapon? In what circumstances?

Recently, in all fields of learning, but particularly in language learning, this traditional view of the teacher-student relationship has been strongly challenged. It is now accepted that learning is a complex process, and does not consist simply of the transmission of knowledge. Teaching has come to be seen as letting learners learn. Teachers have been encouraged to come down off the pedestal that has often been provided for them. The fact that students are also customers in many cases has also been important: if they do not learn, (or do not feel that they are learning) they are not satisfied; they want their money back or they go to another school. So for many schools nowadays it has become financially important to put the accent on good learning.

Another reason why the emphasis should be shifted from teaching to learning is the long-term nature of language learning. It never really stops. This is especially true of a second language: very few people ever achieve native-speaker level. But, even though you will still be learning, the teacher will not always be there. All students must accept that, sooner or later, the teacher will walk out of the door for the last time and from then on the students are on their own.

Thus it could be that teachers who set themselves up as oracles – with the answer to every question, and a correction for every mistake – do their students a grave disservice. Surely it is better to make the students autonomous and independent before the teacher leaves them forever? For those who would dismiss this as a currently fashionable idea, we would quote Cicero, nearly two thousand years ago: *Most commonly the authority of them that teach hinders them that would learn.*

TASK 4

What is your idea of a teacher? Put these twelve possibilities in order of importance for you:

FRIEND	INFORMATION-GIVER
ADVISER	AUTHORITY FIGURE
WITCHDOCTOR	JUDGE
STAR	HERO
HELPER	REFERENCE BOOK
ENEMY	SOUNDING BOARD

Now ask the students in your class to do the same.

Are the results the same as yours, or different?

If you don't like the idea of asking your students, can you say why not? Are you afraid their opinion is going to be embarrassing?

1.3 How do we learn a second language?

If only we knew! Before you read any further, look at the box:

TASK 5 ――――――――――――――――

> Sometimes, teachers forget how they learnt a language.
>
> Think about a language you know very well apart from your own. Which of these factors were important in the process of your learning it? Mark each one *Yes* or *No*.
>
> **Hearing the language on the TV**
>
> **Doing a course at night school**
>
> **Going to a country where it was spoken**
>
> **Having a very good teacher**
>
> **Practising it a lot**
>
> **Learning the grammar formally**
>
> **Picking it up 'on the street'**
>
> **Thinking about it a lot and working it out**
>
> **Liking the lifestyle that goes with it**
>
> **Listening to songs in the language**
>
> **Making friends with someone who spoke the language**
>
> **Learning by heart**
>
> **Something else (write it down)**
>
> Now compare your answers with a colleague.

The state of our knowledge of how we learn a second language is still very elementary. We can rarely say, as learners, *If I do this, then I will learn more quickly* or, as teachers, *If I ask my students to do that, they will learn better.* We can make informed guesses, learn from experience, and from what writers have told us: but the questions above may have shown you that language learning is a highly individual experience, with each student learning in a different way.

One thing, however, is common to all learners of a language, whether it is your first language (L1), or a foreign language (L2): they all make mistakes.

TASK **6** ———————————————

What is your reaction to the statement *All learners of a language make mistakes?*

Write it here:

_____

_____

_____

_____

_____

Babies do it, secondary school students do it, adults do it. Mistakes are an inescapable fact of language learning. The fact that babies do it is, for us, an interesting phenomenon; not because we necessarily believe that L1-learning and L2-learning are similar, but because it indicates that mistakes are natural. More than that, it indicates that mistakes are part of the learning process: not wrong turnings on the road towards mature language use, but actually part of the road itself.

Most people now believe that, given any particular first language, all normal babies will learn the structures of that language in more or less the same order, and at more or less the same speed. In other words, they have a syllabus inside their heads, a so-called 'internal syllabus', and it is difficult or impossible to get a baby to learn in a different order.

TASK 7

Listen to a recording of your most advanced students talking naturally. Do not correct them. Make a list of the mistakes which you consider 'beginners' mistakes'. Do they tend to be similar from one person to another and/or one nationality to another? If they do, what implications does that have for teaching? If they don't, what explanation can be offered?

One of the obvious conclusions of this is that mistakes are an integral part of language-learning and language use. They are inevitable. The teacher or the student may be able to eliminate them to a certain extent – though, as we shall see later, with possible unhelpful effects – but they may never be eliminated altogether.

However, it is possible to go further than that. One idea that may be fruitful to pursue is this: many mistakes should not be eliminated at all, they should be encouraged! If this shocks you, read on...

TASK 8

Write down two or three reasons why you think mistakes should be encouraged.

1.4 Three reasons for encouraging mistakes

It is now accepted that a very important factor in learning a new language, both for babies learning an L1 and all students of an L2, is that of hypothesis-forming. What is this? Basically, the sequence of events is as follows: The baby or L2-learner:

- is exposed to a lot of language

- subconsciously forms ideas – or hypotheses – about how the language works

- puts these ideas into practice by trying out language
- receives new information, that is, is exposed to more language
- changes the original ideas to fit the new information
- tries out the new ideas

and the whole cycle repeats again and again.

It is clear that sometimes the learner will find the right idea straightaway. For example, a learner hears that the negative of *could* is *couldn't*, so when s/he hears *should*, s/he assumes the negative is *shouldn't* – which it is.

It is equally clear that learners often do not hit on the right idea at first. Perhaps they hear verbs like *asked* or *arrived* or *passed* which seem to end in a /t/ or a /d/ sound. When they come to talk about the past, it is natural enough to experiment with *I buyed a teddy this morning.*

Usually parents find this kind of 'mistake' amusing, where perhaps a teacher would find it worrying! It is clear that the word *buyed*, used by a baby, indicates that the baby has learnt the basic rule of past tense formation. In other words, **the mistake is evidence of learning.** What the baby has not learnt – yet – is all the exceptions. So the mistake here is evidence that the learner is moving forward, and has reached an intermediate stage:

Stage 1   **Stage 2**   **Stage 3**

Children's speech is littered with language of this kind. Here are some more examples:

You'd bettern't do that!

I didn't got no sweets.

Daddy gone shops, isn't it?

If you listen to somebody learning a second language, you will hear many similar examples as the learner follows a similar path. (We are not concerned with whether or not it is exactly the same path, but it is certainly similar.)

TASK 9

Listen to your lesson tape. Listen particularly to a part of the lesson where the students are doing a conversation-type activity. Note down all the examples of mistakes due to hypothesis-forming. How did you react to these mistakes?

If it is true that an L2-learner goes through these stages, it must also be true that any behaviour on the teacher's part which hinders the guesses, including wrong ones, will also hinder the process of learning. If the students do not make hypotheses, they will be reduced to copying or imitating the language that they hear from other people – often only the teacher! As a result their language can only be impoverished. They make less progress, because they are unable to create and formulate new sentences of their own.

This means that, in some way, teachers have to allow the students room to make guesses, experiment, and be creative with the language. They have to have the opportunity to make mistakes.

TASK 10

What has just been said is an opinion, not a fact. Do you agree with it? If you don't, why don't you? If you do, what room do you allow your students to make guesses about the language? Ask your colleagues what they think.

To give this room for experimentation to students is a matter of attitude as much as methodology. The teacher's attitude and behaviour are very important. The idea that mistakes are a natural and essential part of learning must be transmitted to the students. If the teacher does not believe it, the students will not either. An obvious implication is that teachers must not leap on 'the mistake' when students try out a new piece of language that happens to be wrong. If they hear a student say

I don't can open the door.

they should recognise that the student is hypothesizing from

I don't like...

I don't want...

They should smile, give encouragement, and **react to the message** by saying, perhaps, *Why not?* or *I see what you mean.* Remember that your reaction is much more than what you **say**; how do you look , or move? What about your tone of voice? If students are criticised for trying, they will stop trying.

TASK 11

Two questions to consider at this point:

1. Listen to your lesson tape. What do you do when a student tries out a piece of language which happens to be wrong? Would your reaction be described as

 a. encouraging

 b. discouraging

 c. neutral?

2. Is it possible to convey to the student that the sentence was 'wrong' without discouraging them from trying again another time? How?

Write down two ideas.

The behaviour described on page 15 might be called forming hypotheses 'internally', because it is made **inside** a language, it is formed from examples in the same language. Another kind of hypothesis-forming is from your first language to the language you are learning.

Let us imagine that a foreign learner arrives in an English-speaking country, and is talking to somebody on the third day of their visit. They want to say: *I have been here for two days.*

Unfortunately the syllabus of their course book has not reached the present perfect yet! What is this student to do? They can

a. keep quiet

b. use their own language as a basis for speaking in English

c. make some other guess.

But if the student chooses the last alternative, what guarantee have they got that the guess will be right? At least their own language provides a chance: if such a form exists in their own L1, perhaps it exists in English too? So the student (if s/he's feeling adventurous) says, perhaps: *I am here from two days.*

Teachers have tended to be very severe on this kind of mistake. *They just assume it will be the same in English!* they cry in desperation. But it sometimes is! *I have never seen that film* in English is *Je n'ai jamais vu ce-film là* in French, *Non ho mai visto quel film,* in Italian, or *No he nunca visto aquel film* in Spanish. All these examples use the same tense form, same auxiliary, and the same demonstrative. The language being learnt is not always different from the L1 – so a guess based on the student's own language has a better chance of being right than a random guess.

In other words, the L1 is a **resource** which the student uses when, for some reason, the L2 form eludes them. Equally, other languages – an L3 – can be called upon, a habit which seems to us to be natural, intelligent and resourceful, and so to be encouraged.

TASK 12

People often talk of 'L1 interference', where the mother-tongue of the learner causes some of the mistakes in a second language. In which of these areas do you think this is strongest?

a. pronunciation
b. vocabulary
c. structure

If L1 interference is important, how do we explain the fact that, at least in structure, all students, whatever their L1, find certain points difficult?

Teachers at this point sometimes say: *Bah! Well, they shouldn't try and say things they haven't learnt yet.* Usually what they mean is: they shouldn't try to say things **I** haven't taught them! This is not very helpful if we are trying to encourage independent learners!

TASK 13

Do you agree? How far should students be allowed to say what they like in the classroom? Is the classroom the same thing as the outside world?

Teachers tend to see mistakes only in terms of what the student actually says. These could be called 'mistakes of commission'. Another way of looking at mistakes is in terms of what the student did not attempt to say – in other words, 'mistakes of omission'.

Why should it matter what the student did not say? Simply because, if language is communication, then non-communication is a kind of mistake. If the student wants to say something, but is prevented, that is surely unsatisfactory. One of the reasons they do not say it is because they are worried about the possibility of making a mistake.

17

Here is an example. A teacher asks the class what they think of bullfighting. Carlos says:

I no like it. Is orrible. But exist since a long time, is very important for Espanish people....

Maria says:

I don't know. It's very difficult.

Maybe Maria is thinking 'Actually watching bullfighting is a wonderful experience, and certainly no worse morally than fox-hunting or angling, or whaling....' but she is also thinking 'How on earth can I say all that in English – I'm bound to make a lot of mistakes!' But how long can Maria wait? And what happens when somebody asks her the same question after class has finished?

TASK 14

Think about a class you are teaching at the moment. Rank all the students on a scale from 1 to 10 where 1 would be Carlos in the example above (inaccurate but adventurous and genuinely communicative) and 10 would be Maria (full of interesting ideas, but too careful about her language to be able to express them well).

What strategies can you devise to make Carlos more careful and, perhaps more importantly, Maria more careless/carefree?

One more point about language-learning: its long-term nature. Learning an L2 takes a long time and a lot of patience. Teachers are inclined to confuse short- and long-term objectives. We have to remember that language learners are in constant development – from knowing nothing towards, if not knowing everything, then at least having a working control of the language. But this development is not linear. It fluctuates, even from day to day. Two steps forward, one step back. It seems wrong to correct a student on Wednesday for what they were able to get right on Tuesday.

Language learners are involved in an elaborate process: sometimes the language they produce reflects the point they have reached, but often it does not. **Rather than criticise the product, it may be the teacher's job to aid the process.** After all, students do not usually make mistakes deliberately. Many teachers worry about their students' communication being **defective**: it may be more fruitful to concentrate on ways of making it more **effective**. Concentrate on what is good. Encourage progress. Be patient.

Examples from other kinds of learning may be helpful. It is often the mistake itself which produces or improves the learning. Think about learning to drive: even the best drivers had trouble with the gears or forgot to take off the handbrake when they were learning. Indeed, the very act of grating the gears helped many of us to understand the function of the clutch pedal! The person who never made a mistake, never made anything.

CHAPTER TWO

WHAT IS A MISTAKE?

We said in the introduction that it has been traditional to try and define mistakes, and to categorise them according to their causes. So that there is a range of words, of which 'mistake' is one, to denote various kinds of errors.

We do not believe that the state of such definitions is sufficiently advanced to make distinctions particularly useful. For example, it is common to distinguish between 'mistakes' and 'errors', the former being caused by the learner not putting into practice something they have learned, the latter being caused by the learner trying out something completely new, and getting it wrong.

We believe that this distinction is an academic one: in practice, and especially on the spur of the moment in a class, it is impossible to distinguish between the two. How can we tell what a student has 'learned'? Does that mean things the student has **met**, or things the student has **mastered**? Maybe a student has been taught a lesson during which the word 'library' came up. Did the student learn it? How can we tell? Maybe s/he understood it at the time, and even wrote it down in a notebook – but does that mean the student 'learned' it? Equally, we may say that a student has not 'learned' a word or structure because it has never come up in class – but maybe they heard it on the radio the evening before. We are really talking about whether the student has been taught it or not – a completely different matter. When we asked a colleague *What did you do with the class this morning?*, she replied: *Well, I did the simple past, but I don't know if they did!* Learning is not the same thing as teaching!

In this book, we are going to use just two terms:

Slip. This is wrong language caused by tiredness,

carelessness, nerves etc. In other words, the kind of mistake that anybody, including native-speakers, could make.

Mistake. This is wrong language which a native-speaker would not usually produce, that is, something that only learners of the language produce.

TASK 15

What do you think of the argument that it is impossible in practical terms to trace the causes of mistakes in a classroom situation? Does it assume too much independence on the part of the student?

If you think that the distinction between 'errors' and 'mistakes' is useful, what **practical** implications does it have for

    a. learning?

    b. teaching?

Another distinction which is often made is that of 'covert' mistakes. These are occasions when the learner says something right by accident. An example would be: *We went to some museum and then took the train home.* In the student's L1, *some* is followed by a singular, even when referring to more than one thing – they really mean *some museums.* However, *some museum* is perfectly acceptable English, although it has a slightly different meaning.

TASK 16

How do you react in class to a 'mistake' like this?

Do you attempt to reconstruct the thought patterns of the student, using their L1? Then what do you do?

We discuss the function of the covert mistake, and ways of reacting to it constructively, in chapter 5.

TASK 17

Before you read the next section, answer
this question: what is a mistake?
Discuss your answer with a colleague.

Of course, your idea of what a mistake is depends on who
you are. We asked some language students and teachers.
Here are some of their answers:

To say or write something wrong. (student)

*Everything which is wrong. I can't give details.
There are too many. (student)*

*It depends on circumstances. It could be
something a native speaker wouldn't say
grammatically, something a native-speaker
wouldn't say in a certain situation. It depends on
the audience. The definition of a 'mistake' shifts.
(teacher)*

*A wrong opinion, idea or act because of wrong
information. (student)*

As we can see, teachers and students often believe that a
mistake is somehow 'wrong'. However, the situation is
more complicated than that. Perhaps a useful distinction
here is the one we made earlier between language as a tool
of communication, and language as a system to be studied
on its own, with no relation to real life.

Let us imagine two business people, one German and the
other Japanese, arguing about the price of a product – in
English. One says: *I can't to bring the price down any further.*

It is clear that, as a piece of communication, this
sentence functions well enough – it will not be
misunderstood. If it is wrong, it is because it breaks the
'rules' of the language, in this case the rule that you must
use the infinitive without *to* after modal auxiliary verbs like

can. If, on the other hand, the business person says: *Always my machine cost £450* this offends against communication, since it is not clear (unless the context tells us) whether we are talking about the past or the present. A mistake of communication is always also a mistake of the 'rules' – but the reverse is not true.

Task 18

Think about the phrase 'unless the context tells us'.

How often does the context supply information which actually renders an incomprehensible statement comprehensible?

Listen to your lesson tape – concentrate on a part of an intermediate or advanced class where the students are talking freely. Divide the mistakes into three kinds:

a. ones which don't affect comprehensibility

b. ones which are comprehensible from context

c. ones which are not comprehensible

Are you surprised by the results?

How did the students react to the mistakes?

What implications does this have for your teaching?

Of course, there will always be grey areas, but this distinction between intelligibility and non-intelligibility as a way of judging a mistake is very useful. It looks at mistakes from the point of view of their **effect**, not of their **cause**. In this way, it reflects real-life language use. A natural user of a second language (as opposed to one who uses it only in the classroom) will tell you that people in the real world are never particularly worried about mistakes until they impede communication.

In fact, it is teachers who are worried by mistakes (and particularly non-native-speaker teachers). They are worried about them even if, or especially if, they are merely ones which offend the 'code'. If you show the same set of imperfect compositions to separate groups of teachers and non-teachers, the non-teachers will praise the amount the students have managed to get right, while the teachers concentrate on what is wrong! And, we should repeat, teachers tend to concentrate their correcting tendencies on the mistake of commission, and forget about what has been omitted .

A further point is that non-native teachers tend to be severest of all on mistakes. This is entirely understandable, given that they are often less sure of their own English. They themselves were probably taught by a teacher who believed that 'good English' **means** 'free of mistakes'. We discuss non-native teaching more in chapter 9.

TASK 19

Grade the mistakes in the following sentences from 5 - 0 where 5 is a very serious mistake, and 0 is no mistake at all. You must define for yourself what 'serious' means.

1. She asked me where did I come from.
2. The book was into the bag.
3. The problem was that the door wasn't keyed.
4. He's fond of cooking himself and for me.
5. A few people and I was looking for the mysterious monster.
6. Did you went there alone?
7. The people paniced and some of them runed away.
8. She was about herself very sensible.
9. We visit Torquay last weekend.
10. I like the city very much, because it is lively and expected about the future.

Now turn to p119 for a discussion of the results.*

One final point. One of the teachers in the survey above made a useful point: a mistake depends on the audience. The importance of a mistake in real life depends on the situation in which it occurs. If a doctor is instructing a nurse to make up a prescription, the pronunciation mistake that confuses 40 for 30 could be fatal! A foreigner who is planning to marry an English girl might find, on meeting the in-laws, that a mistake of grammar could count for less than one of register. *Pass the salt* might be less appreciated than *Could you to pass salt, please?* Embarrassment and confusion are the two keys to linguistic behaviour outside the classroom – much more powerful than the teacher's arbitrary interventions. Also, grammar (or structure) may be less important than vocabulary or pronunciation or register. Grammar might also be less important than teachers think.

*This exercise is based upon an article by Hughes and Lascaratou: 'Competing criteria for Error Gravity' in ELTJ vol 36/3.

CHAPTER THREE

TEACHER AND STUDENT BEHAVIOUR

> **TASK 20**
>
> Answer these questions as honestly as you can.
> 1. How much do you correct students?
> 2. Why do you do it?

3.1 The problems of the heavy corrector

In our experience, the main problems in a class dominated by correction belong to the students, not to the teacher. These are:

1. Teacher-dominance – everything is focussed on the teacher, the students are subsidiary figures, and learning is subjugated to teaching.

2. Lack of 'space' – the students' creativity is stifled, because accuracy is valued much more highly than fluency or imagination

3. Lack of independent thought – the students' linguistic brains work along pre-set lines. They tend to come up with fixed phrases and are unable to make new and original language.

4. Caution – students tend to take a long time formulating sentences, and are obsessed with the final result being correct.

5. Tension – students are worried about making mistakes.

6. Internal struggle on the part of the teacher – often teachers do not want to correct heavily, but feel they must; and cannot think of a way of escaping from the situation.

7. Teachers end up correcting right to right, or even right to wrong!

TASK 21

If you are a 'heavy corrector', do you believe that your students (and you) have these problems?

3.2 The problems of the non-corrector

These, on the other hand, tend to be centred on the teacher, not the student. Often, they are non-pedagogic, even administrative, because they are to do with student expectations.

1. Guilt – teachers feel that they should correct, even if they are not convinced of its value.

2. Complaints 1 – students often complain about being corrected too little (they rarely complain openly about being corrected too much). Sometimes they go to the teacher to complain, but at other times to people above the teacher.

3. Complaints 2 – parents and school authorities are often unhappy about a non-correcting teacher, especially when the teacher is preparing the students for an exam. (Exams are often accuracy-based.)

4. Image – others tend to think you are lazy, irresponsible or incompetent.

5. Student-anxiety – students begin to wonder if the teacher knows what s/he is doing.

TASK 22

If you are a 'non-corrector', do you recognise these problems. What others would you list?

3.3 How can we cope with these problems?

If you are an 'over-corrector':

- correct less!

- correct at specific points of your lesson

- give your students more room

- correct better – use better or different techniques

TASK 23

How could you correct less?

At what points of the lesson could correcting be reduced?

In what ways could you give students more room?

If you are a non-corrector:

- be prepared to do more 'public relations'
- take students into your confidence
- be prepared to compromise sometimes

TASK 24

Imagine that you are going to teach a group of adult students for a longish period. You have decided, as an experiment, that you will not correct them at all. How will you explain this to them? What objections do you think they will make? How could you link this in with exploring the nature of language-learning with them?

Let us imagine that the class is going to take an exam at the end of the course which demands a high degree of accuracy. How will this affect

a. your experiment?

b. your explanations to the students?

Would things be very different if you were to teach a class of 35 thirteen-year-olds in a State school?

We said in chapter 1 that there is an enormous variety of types of student. Factors like age, nationality and background play a large part. As far as mistakes and mistake-correction are concerned, we can say that most students **expect** teachers to correct them, because that is the traditional view of what a language teacher does, and they come from educational backgrounds where teachers correct a lot. In particular, it is rare to find teachers in secondary schools who do not correct, so, for example, adult learners will expect it.

This does not necessarily mean that they want it. We can identify two very clear groups: those who believe that correction is good for them, and want a lot of it, and those who get frustrated by the amount they are corrected when they are really interested in expressing themselves. These two groups of students often find themselves in the same class.

TASK 25

List all the students in one of your intermediate classes. Which of the two categories above do they fall into? Or are they somewhere in between? How do you know?

Compare your answers with a colleague who teaches the same class. Do you have the same answers? Why? Why not?

If you find yourself faced with a class that insists you correct them all the time – as has happened to the authors on occasion – you might like to take them at their word. Students who are corrected literally **every** time they make a mistake very soon get bored with it, especially when they are really trying to communicate. They don't usually last more than a couple of minutes!

3.4 The Psychology of Correction

Correction has a number of possible psychological effects on students, and what affects one student badly affects another very positively. Here is a list we made:

1. Frustration – 'My teacher isn't listening to **me** but my language'

'My teacher interrupts me when I

29

really want to say something.'

'My teacher never corrects me.'

2. Discouragement – 'This language is too hard for me.'

'I can't make any progress because no-one tells me what's right and what's wrong.'

3. Satisfaction – 'My teacher is increasing my accuracy.'

'I know I can try things out, and check with the teacher if they are right or not.'

4. Confidence – 'This teacher seems to know what she's doing.'

5. Fear – 'I mustn't speak unless I know what I'm going to say is right.'

TASK 26

It is difficult to assess the real effect you have on your students. Ask a colleague to observe you and find out the following:
1. What is the predominant atmosphere in the class?
2. What is the primary effect of your correcting (if any)? Is it one of the list above, or something else again?
3. What changes could be made in the amount of correction (not the technique of correcting) to improve this effect?
Try these questions out on the students too if you have the confidence!

Most teachers lie somewhere between the two extremes we outlined at the start of this chapter. Although we have met teachers who never correct, and we have met teachers who correct by bringing students to the front of the class and forcing them to repeat the phrase again and again until the student either gets it right or breaks down in tears, most teachers are somewhere in between. Their problems are a mixture of the problems of the two extremes.

Lots of teachers have worked out that some correction is useful for a number of reasons: students are so varied in their backgrounds, their needs and their expectations, or because their learning styles are so different, or because it is politic.

It is clear that confidence is a key word. Some students gain confidence from being allowed to express themselves without being picked up for every mistake; some gain confidence from knowing very strictly the limits of what is right and wrong. The one thing that can bring these two seemingly opposed groups together is **technique.** Students have to realise – teachers have to let students know – that mistakes:

a. are necessary

b. are acceptable

c. will be dealt with in a non-judgmental, supportive and effective way.

Bad mistake-management is worse than none at all. But good mistake-management helps everybody. Good mistake-management enables teachers to continue to maintain a professional position in front of students, colleagues and authorities alike, whilst avoiding the problems, both didactic and psychological, which over-correction, or poor correction, brings. The following chapters discuss what good mistake-management might be.

CHAPTER FOUR

ORAL MISTAKES – PRIORITIES

4.1 Fluency and Accuracy

The traditional model for deciding a teacher's priorities when it comes to reacting to a student's oral mistakes is based upon the distinction between accuracy and fluency. This is substantially a circular argument because our definitions of accuracy and fluency are often based upon our attitudes to mistakes:

accuracy work is defined as that part of the lesson where students are encouraged to make their utterances as near to a native-speaker's as possible – which is usually taken as necessitating more intense correction.

fluency is defined as that part of the lesson where students work on their capacity to communicate within the language, generally a period free of correction. Most teachers have adopted these terms and some textbooks have even started labelling their exercises according to whether they are principally orientated towards fluency or accuracy.

We believe that these labels are teachers' conveniences, and useful for that reason. They are really ways of describing interaction in class, rather than types of exercise. They are indicative of states of mind rather than types of activity. You can set up a 'fluency-activity' – where the students are asked to talk freely without corrections – but if the students do not believe in the importance of fluency, they will not suddenly speak fluently by doing that activity. If they are interested in being accurate at all times, then it will be an 'accuracy-activity' as far as they are concerned.

This seems to us to be a crucial point to remember: it is the **student's aims** which are important. It is very unlikely that the student is thinking in terms of fluency or accuracy.

TASK 27

> Did you learn a foreign language at school? If so, have you ever thought about your fluency or accuracy in that language (even if you do not use those exact words)? Did you ever think about these factors before you became a language teacher?

The problem with accuracy and fluency is that they impose a two-sided view of language, when language is, in fact, multi-sided. For example, most teachers see accuracy as something you work on when you are freshest – so we have accuracy work at the start of the lesson, and fluency work at the end; we have grammar exercises in the morning and conversation classes in the afternoon. Songs and games are labelled 'fluency' and pushed to Friday afternoon. But students do not see things in the same way. Recently, we heard of a school where the students were asked to design the syllabus for the following week – and they chose songs on Monday morning. The lesson was a great success.

Maybe we should start looking at accuracy and fluency only as **part** of the process – what about other factors such as imagination and creativity?

TASK 28

> Make a list of other factors that go to make up the whole language learning experience. We have suggested 'imagination' and 'creativity': how many more would you include?

Let us imagine, however, that we are in a phase of the lesson where some work on mistakes will be necessary. Should every mistake be dealt with in some way?

We have talked in chapter 3 of the long-term considerations – the psychological effect on the students, the increased dependence that students might have on the teacher when s/he corrects a lot, and so on. Most teachers, however, have a list of short-term considerations which influence them too.

Task 29

Make a list of the short-term considerations you use in class when you decide whether to let a mistake go or not.
Write these considerations down on a piece of paper. Then listen to your lesson tape.
Do you really follow your list?

Here is our list. We have put it in order of importance, with the most important first, but every teacher will have a different order.

1. Does the mistake affect communication?
2. Are we concentrating on accuracy at the moment?
3. Is it really wrong? Or is it my imagination?
4. Why did the student make the mistake?
5. Is it the first time the student has spoken for a long time?
6. Could the student react badly to my correction?
7. Have they met this language point in the current lesson?
8. Is it something the students have already met?
9. Is this a mistake that several students are making?
10. Would the mistake irritate somebody?
11. What time is it?
12. What day is it?
13. What's the weather like?

TASK 30

Look at no 4. Think about this critically. Is it possible to answer this question? If it is, how?

Look at no 6. What might 'badly' mean?

Look at no 8. What do you understand by 'already met'? During this course? In their life?

Look at no 9. If several students are making the same mistake, what implications are there?

4.2 Why has the student made the mistake?

We have already said that we do not find the distinction between 'errors' and 'mistakes' useful for the practical purposes of classroom teaching. However, we do believe it is useful and instructive for teachers to ask **why** a mistake has been made.

a. Was it a piece of language experimentation or hypothesis-forming such as we have seen in previous chapters? This experimenting might be of a linguistic kind:

T Do you think it's going to rain tomorrow?

S I don't think so. I heard on the radio.

T What about you, Francois?

S I don't hope so. I'm going skiing!

Here the student simply hypothesizes that *hope* behaves in the same way as *think*. Equally, the experiment could be of a non-linguistic kind:

T Did you enjoy the school trip yesterday?

S Oh, I liked it. Because we don't must go to school!

T Oh, I see what you mean. You didn't have to come to school.

S No, that was great.

Here the student is trying to be amusing – to use language for a real purpose. That is important. The student's adventurousness has produced a complicated mistake. We do not want the student to lose the positive attitude s/he has, so correction may not be appropriate. See the next section for more ideas about this.

TASK 31

> Listen to your lesson tape or ask a colleague to observe. How much do the students experiment with the language? If the answer is 'Not much', how do you feel about that? Can you think of ways of encouraging students to do it more?
>
> If they do experiment, what is your actual reaction (as opposed to how you think you react)?
>
> What happens in other classes? Observe one or two colleagues teaching – how do they react to linguistic experimenting by students? Are their students more or less cautious than yours? Why?

b. Was the mistake in fact a slip? Was it just the result of tiredness or forgetfulness?

c. Did the student get the mistake from the teacher, or the material? Not as silly as it sounds! Look at this dialogue:

> **T** Ilse, ask Kurt what time the train leaves.
>
> **S** Kurt, what time the train leaves?

Here the student has simply repeated the structure used by the teacher: in the student's own language, it might be perfectly possible to use the same word order in both kinds of question.

Unusual stress and intonation may occur:

T My name's Joanne. What's **your** name?

S (later in same class) What's **your** name?

If the teacher stresses the correction itself, the student may do the same:

S Where do Michael live?

T Not do, but **does**.

S Ah, yes. Where **does** Michael live?

TASK **32**

Listen to your lesson tape. Are any of the students' mistakes due to what you have said (or the way you said it)? Are they caused by something in the materials you are using?

4.3 Is it appropriate to today's lesson?

One model for lesson preparation is as follows: every lesson should have an aim. This aim might be linguistic or non-linguistic; it might be a structure, a function, or a skill. If the students make a mistake when working on the aim of the lesson, the mistake should be dealt with. If the mistake is on another point, it can be left. For example, a teacher is working on the past simple with a class. A student says *On Wednesday, I have go to London.*

Since the problem lies with the very point of the lesson, the mistake could be corrected. If the student says *On Wed-nes-day, I went to London*, the mistake is left because the problem is with the pronunciation of *Wednesday*, which is not the focus of the lesson.

Maybe this is extended further – the teacher remembers that the class studied the days of the week recently, so that a correction is justified.

TASK 33

What is your normal practice on this point? Do you concentrate only on mistakes which are the focus of the lesson, or do you tend to correct more widely? Listen to your lesson tape and find out.

How do you react to the idea that only items which are the focus of the lesson should be corrected?

Do you think it's practical? What about the difference between teaching and learning? (Maybe the point of the lesson is something rather different in the students' minds!)

Is it reasonable to expect students to 'learn' something in just one lesson? If it is, how reasonable is it to expect them to remember it in a subsequent lesson? Is that how learning works, in your opinion? Discuss your opinions with a colleague.

4.4 Would the mistake irritate somebody?

Don't forget that teachers are irritated by different things from non-teachers. One of the things that irritates us most about student behaviour is saying 'Hello' when they mean 'Goodbye', but we recognise this is irrational! Try to put yourself in the position of a native-speaker who is not a teacher of EFL.

TASK 34

Make a list of your students' mistakes which irritate you. Are they the same as the ones that irritate your colleagues? How many of them would have the same effect upon a non-teacher?

These priorities are highly subjective. A good rule for the teacher is: be flexible. Your biggest asset is your knowledge of the class, not your knowledge of the language. Treat each student as an individual. **Remember that you don't correct a mistake, you correct a person!**

4.5 Dealing with Covert Mistakes

What is a covert mistake? And how important are they really? A covert mistake is when the student says something which is correct, but is not what they meant. Two examples might be:

How long are you in Cambridge?

If the company will guarantee delivery, we will order large quantities.

These two examples are fundamentally different. In the first example, the student actually means *How long have you been in Cambridge?* In other words, they are talking about the past, but the person addressed will assume they are talking about the future. This is a misunderstanding.

In the second, the student puts *will* into the *if-clause*, even though normally, we would use a present tense: in fact, in this case, it is possible to use *will* in the sense of *if the company is willing to... .* In another case, the same student would produce something like *If the weather will get better, we can play tennis.* but there is still no misunderstanding.

TASK 35

> Listen to your lesson tape, or examine closely a recent piece of written work by your students. How many covert mistakes can you find? Which of the two categories above do they fall into?

Our view is that covert mistakes matter as much or as little as any kind of mistake: if they block communication, they do matter, but otherwise perhaps not. One thing to remember is that covert mistakes can be self- correcting:

A How long are you in Oxford?

B Oh, probably a couple of years, but I don't know.

A ? (A tries again.)

But this is not always true:

A How long are you in Cambridge?

B Two weeks.

A Oh, that's interesting.

It is more important to give the students information about the covert mistake (like any mistake) rather than necessarily leap in with a correction – but only if the point is genuinely useful, and only if the student is not going to be corrected automatically by the subsequent conversation.

TASK 36

'Giving the students information' about a mistake does not necessarily mean the teacher explaining the grammar point to the students in the class. Look at the following covert mistakes and decide:

a. what did the student mean?

b. how serious is the mistake?

c. how would you give further information to the students to help them to understand the problems involved?

1. I like film very much.
2. A man ran to me and pushed me.
3. I was really shocked after this accident, but luckily I am healthy.
4. Actually, he's in the other room.
5. Will you come to the school tomorrow?

You can find our comments on these examples in the Commentary, page 121.

In conclusion, we feel that covert mistakes should be managed in the same way as any other mistakes – as an opportunity to extend and develop the student's English.

CHAPTER FIVE

ORAL MISTAKES – TECHNIQUES

5.1 Introduction

Here is an example (actually heard by us in a class) of the way many teachers react to mistakes by their students when speaking:

    T What about house prices in the city centre?

    S I don't know exactly how much cost a house in city centre, but I think it's very expensive.

    T Yeah. Don't forget you have to invert verb and subject in an indirect question.

    S Sorry?

    T ....so you say '...how much a house costs...'

    S Oh, yes.

This kind of correction worries us, well-intentioned and pleasantly carried out though it was. We are not convinced it is either effective or helpful. There are several reasons:

1. The teacher stops the student in the middle of what he is saying, which can be frustrating and discouraging.

2. The student concerned is not involved at all in the process of correcting, and therefore learns little or nothing.

3. The other students are sitting there, doing nothing.

4. A student placed in this situation will possibly feel resentment and humiliation, building up a resistance to the teacher, the language, or both.

5. The teacher uses phrases about the language such as 'invert', 'indirect questions' etc which will be useful to only a limited number of students.

6. The teacher is doing most of the talking.

TASK 37———————

To think about:

a. Do you correct like this? If you do, would you agree with the criticisms above? Why/why not?

b. What problems does the use of words like *verb* and *noun* bring up? Where do you stop? We can label forms like *phrasal verbs* and *prepositions*, but how useful are labels like *demonstrative* and *subject/object?*

c. Can you think of two or three situations where the use of grammatical language like *invert* might be useful to the students?

When have you found it useful to employ words like this?

This section of the book is devoted to exploring different ways of managing mistakes. We prefer the word 'managing' to 'correcting', because we believe that the outcome of a mistake should be more or less the same as the outcome of a correct sentence: the student makes progress.

The first thing to point out is that it is useless for a teacher to adopt a style of teaching with which they feel uncomfortable. The aim of this book is not to impose a teaching style on anybody, but to encourage exploring new styles. For example, we discuss the use of gesture to help students. Many teachers feel *I'm not the sort of person to wave my arms about* – but have you tried? We believe that every teacher has to gather a repetoire of techniques and strategies, from which they can choose when a particular situation arises. We are not talking about gimmicks to get the attention of the students, but looking for non-judgmental ways of indicating that, although mistakes are acceptable, there are times when we can and do want to work on them.

One of the commonest problems, exemplified by the dialogue above, is that teachers often feel obliged to do the correcting.

TASK 38

If the teacher does not correct, who does? Think of at least two other people in the class who could correct instead of the teacher.

The advantages of students doing the correction are obvious:

- they feel more involved.

- they learn to be more independent.

- the feeling of co-operation is greater.

- it reduces the time the teacher spends talking.

TASK 39

Look at this dialogue in class, using peer correction.

Gustavo   What about to go swimming?
Teacher   (Gestures the presence of a mistake and repetition)
Gustavo   What about to go swimming?
Teacher   Not quite...Martina, can you help Gustavo?
Martina   What about going swimming?
Teacher   Right! OK, Gustavo? Can you say that?
Gustavo   What about going swimming?
Teacher Good!

Would this kind of dialogue be possible in your class? If not, why not? Do you have objections to this kind of interaction? Why?

5.2 How can I show the students they have made a mistake?

Gestures: **a.** open hand, rotating wrist, palm down (see fig.1)

b. a wave of the finger (see fig.2)

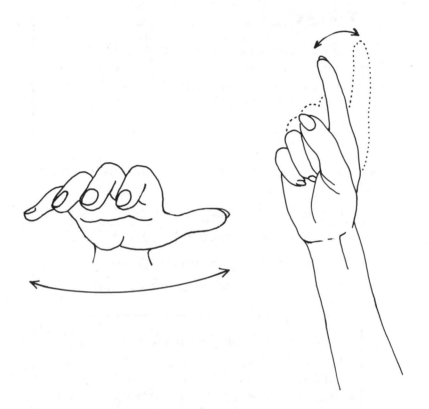

FIGURE 1   FIGURE 2

Facial expressions: **a.** shaking the head

b. frowning

c. doubtful expression

Non-verbal sounds: **a.** "Mmmmmmh" with doubtful intonation

b. "Errrr..."

Simple phrases: **a.** "Nearly....",

"Not quite...."

"Good, but...."

TASK 40

Have you used all these techniques to indicate a mistake?

If you haven't: Try them out. Do you find them helpful? Do they save time, or do they only confuse the students?

If you have: What are their advantages and disadvantages? Are they all equally useful? Do you use others which are not listed above? Do you think any in the above list should be avoided? Why, and in which circumstances?

In particular, can the use of gesture risk offence?

What rules would you lay down for someone using gestures for the first time with a class? Think about both clarity and consistency.

How would all these techniques work with

a. large classes

b. classes of children?

If you feel they would not work well, how could they be adapted for these types of classes?

5.3 How can I show them *where* the mistake is?

Finger technique. This involves the teacher representing each word of the sentence with the fingers of one hand, and with the index finger of the other hand, tapping or holding the 'incorrect' (fig 3) or 'missing' (fig 4)finger/word.

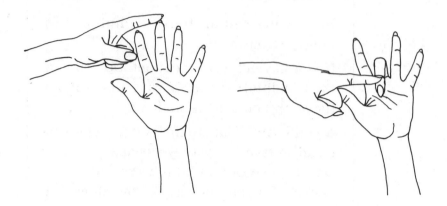

FIGURE 3   FIGURE 4

Simple Phrases: a. Indicate verbally which word is wrong:

> **S** Yesterday I go to the doctor.
>
> **T** Not 'go' but.... (rising intonation, pause)
>
> or Go?

b. Repeat as far as, but not including, the mistake, and then let the student continue:

> **S** Last summer, I went in Scotland.
>
> **T** Last summer, I went.... (pause)
>
> **S** to Scotland.
>
> **T** Right.

TASK **41**

Have you used these techniques? What effect do they have? What part of the lesson, and during what kinds of activities, have you found them most useful? Can you add to the list?

5.4 Indicating the kind of mistake

Gesture: All teachers have their own series of gestures, but here are some that are commonly used:

a. Past time (for example, *Do you see the film yesterday?*):
Try the over-the-shoulder hand or thumb movement to show past time rather than present time (see fig.5)

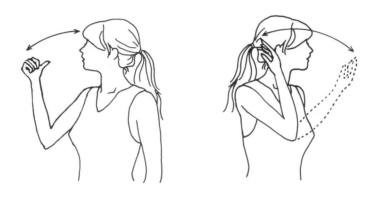

FIGURE 5

b. Future time *(Tomorrow he meets his mother at six):*
Point into the distance in front of you, or roll the hand forward in the air. (see fig.6)

FIGURE 6

c. Contractions *(It is not an interesting book)*
Link index fingers in front of you, or bring thumb and index finger together (see fig.7)

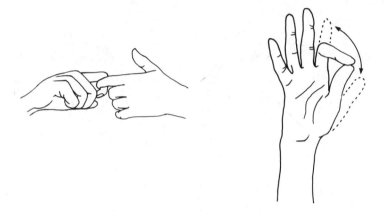

FIGURE 7A   FIGURE 7B

d. Word order *(I like very much the cinema.)*
Cross over your arms in front of you. (fig.8)

FIGURE 8

e. Pronunciation

Cup your hand behind your ear, as if you haven't heard properly.

f. Intonation

Sweep the hand horizontally in front of you, using the movement of the hand up or down to show what is wrong, or what the right intonation should be.

In general, humour can be used, without sarcasm, for some students to indicate an unsuitable tone of voice. For example, if the student sounds very aggressive, you can pretend to salute, or tremble with fear; if the student sounds bored, you could pretend to yawn.

TASK 42

Would this kind of technique work with your students?

If not, why not? Can you think of situations where this kind of humour might not go down very well?

What other light-hearted ways have you used for a similar effect?

5.5 Pretending to misunderstand

This has the double advantage of involving no criticism on the part of the teacher, and also resembling what happens in real life. Here are some examples:

    S She went on holiday with your husband.
    T My husband????
    S No, sorry, her husband.

    S I watch TV on Saturday night.
    T What – **every** Saturday night?
    S No, no, I watched...

S We went to Corfu on a big sheep.

T That must have been uncomfortable.

S (sighs) Ship, ship, ship, ship....

See also the section on reformulation below.

> **TASK 43**
>
> Not all teachers and students are comics. How do you feel about the dialogues above? How do you use humour - if at all - to manage mistakes?
>
> Do you think it has a place? Observe other teachers and see what they do.

5.6 Repeating in Context

Often the very act of correcting changes the nature of the original sentence, particularly when we are talking about stress. In fact, much real-life correcting is done using stress alone:

A His telephone number's 65789.

B 65689, you mean.

In the classroom, this leads to the situation where the corrected sentence has an artificial stress. For example, in the sentence *I'm going to Brazil*, the word *to* would normally be pronounced /tə/. But when you are correcting, you are likely to give it its full value and pronounce it /tuː/.

Many teachers believe, therefore, that you should ask students to repeat the original sentence with the original stress and intonation. For the above example, the dialogue would run:

S I'm going in Brazil.

T (gestures mistakes in third word)

S To?

T Good! Repeat the whole sentence.

S   I'm going to Brazil.

T   Good!

> ## TASK 44
>
> Some teachers dislike the above technique intensely. Do you?
>
> Do your colleagues? Why?
>
> Do you think that correction produces artificial stress, or is the problem exaggerated?

5.7   Echoing

Many teachers believe it is bad practice to 'echo' students when they make a mistake. For example:

S   I am born in Tokyo.

T   I am born in Tokyo?

Why is it considered bad practice?

1.   It often sounds as if the teacher is trying to make fun of the student.

2.   It is hard to say if the teacher is actually indicating a mistake in the language – or just sounding doubtful about the content of what was said. The students might go away from the class thinking the form is right.

3.   The teacher is giving no guidance about why it might be wrong.

> ## TASK 45
>
> It is well-known that teachers do not realise they are echoing! Listen to your lesson tape, and see if you do it.
>
> Do you agree that echoing is bad practice? Why? Why not? Can you think of any reasons why it might be helpful?

5.8 Reformulation

The techniques we have discussed above might be called 'traditional'. They still rely on the teacher having to point out to the students where and how they are wrong, and getting the student to say the correct language. The possible long-term disadvantages of this approach were discussed earlier. However, learning a second language is usually on a shorter timetable than a first language, and we are under an obligation to provide as much feedback, as quickly as possible, to the students on their performance. As we said above, students also expect this feedback.

This means we need to think about ways of providing feedback on the students' performance without the drawbacks noted earlier. One way of doing this is through reformulation.

Reformulation attempts to imitate the way in which real-life correction happens. People in the street or in shops do not usually go around tapping their fingers or waving their arms in front of them to indicate a mistake has been made. Often, they reformulate what the speaker said in a correct form. Sometimes they do this without realising there was a mistake.

To do this in the classroom is a real skill, and an important one for teachers to develop. It is particularly important if you have been used to more overt forms of correction. A typical dialogue might go like this:

S Yes, and on Saturday I go to Bath on trip...

T You're going to Bath? That'll be nice.

S Yes, I going to Bath, and we see the Romanic Baths.

T Have you seen the Roman Baths before?

S No, this is first time.

T What, the very first time?

S Yes, I never see before.

T Right, so Sonia's going to Bath to see the Roman Baths... And what's anybody else doing?

The success of reformulation depends on two principles:
1. Progress in second language learning is gradual, and often indirect: it may not be Sonia who picks up the difference between *Roman* and *Romanic*, but another

student altogether. It is based on the idea that learning takes place all the time, not just when the teacher is explicitly 'teaching'.

2. Students need to be interested in the subject matter – if they are not involved in what they hear, they will find learning harder.

Some linguists, notably the American Stephen Krashen, have suggested that the language which is truly useful to the learner is unconsciously **acquired by understanding language to which the learner is exposed**. It has even been suggested that formally 'learned' language is often not of use in real situations later and that concentration on formal correction and learning may be counter-productive. Even if we do not go as far as this, one of Krashen's principal methodological suggestions may be useful: if a student makes a mistake, the teacher should respond, not necessarily with a 'correction', but should try to expose the student to language just above the student's current level of English – language which, he suggests, is exactly the language which they are ripe to add to their own language reserve.

TASK 46

How do you feel about the idea that formally 'learned' language is of little use in real situations? Think about:

a. when you have studied a foreign language

b. your students learning English.

Does your experience bear these ideas out? Discuss with your colleagues.

What Krashen is suggesting is that, if the teacher responds naturally, reformulating, students are **exposed immediately** to language which they **will understand**, and which is **on the edge of their own current repertoire**. The satisfaction of successful communication will relax the student and 'open' the student to real, long-term learning.

This may be more effective than formal correction, the effectiveness of which is reduced because of the anxiety it may induce, and which 'closes' the student for real long-term learning.

As we pointed out in chapter 1, teachers are often expected to provide correction, especially by the students themselves, and may feel guilty about ignoring mistakes altogether. Reformulation provides a way in which teachers can **react** to a mistake without direct correction. In this way teachers maintain their professional position in the eyes of students and also increase the flexibility of their response to mistakes. In a helpful phrase Peter Wilberg has remarked (in *One-to-One*, LTP 1989) that a **teacher's responsibility is reponse-ability.** Reformulation might be seen as a discriminating response to mistakes, rather than either ignoring, or blindly correcting them.

TASK 47

Reformulation may not be suitable for all kinds of activities in the class. List those where it might be possible, and those where it might not.

Can you see a place for reformulation in your teaching style? Try it out.

One of the problems with reformulation is that it assumes a basic interaction between the teacher and student. In other words, for the teacher to be able to reformulate what the student says, s/he must be actually talking to the student at the time: it would be clumsy, discouraging and unnatural to interrupt two students talking to each other just in order to reformulate something.

However, teachers talking face to face to students is only one of the various interactions during a lesson. Often the students are talking to each other, with the teacher 'monitoring'. Here the teacher may like to try out two other kinds of mistake-management.

5.9 Automatic Correction

Automatic correction depends on this truth: if the mistake is serious enough to block communication, it will show up automatically (because the person being addressed will not understand) and an effective way of communicating the message can be **negotiated** between the students, to the point where both are satisfied. (If the mistake is not serious enough to block communication, it may well not be worth working on anyway.) However, this is a technique that needs to be taught: whereas in real life it happens naturally, in a classroom, the students often expect the teacher to do all the work. The students need to be introduced to it gradually. So an initial dialogue might go like this:

S1 Teacher!

T Yes?

S1 S2 is trying to say something, but I don't understand.

T OK, S2, say it again.

S2 If I like dance, I say you.

T When are you talking about?

S2 Tomorrow.

T OK, S1, keep asking S2 questions about it.

S1 Do you mean dance in the disco?

S2 Yes, dance tomorrow evening.

S1 Ah, you want to go to the disco tomorrow?

S2 Yes, I tell you tomorrow if I go.

After a number of occasions like this, the students should learn to investigate the meaning of an 'incorrect' utterance themselves, rather than always calling on the teacher to do so, or, just as common, give up. Of course, it requires more time and patience at the start, but may well be more productive in the long run. As we observed earlier, Krashen has suggested that the language which remains useful to learners in the long term has been acquired unconsciously. Other theorists (and our own experience) remind us that language learning is a process, and that trying-learning-forgetting-re-meeting-understanding better- forgetting a bit-revising-forming a new hypothesis – trying again **is** language learning. Often when teachers 'save time', they save **themselves** time in a particular lesson: they do not provide a real short-cut for the learners.

> TASK 48
>
> What problems would the procedure on p55 produce?
>
> In which parts of the lesson would it be possible/impossible? What implications does it have for students' autonomy?
>
> Is it still too teacher-based?
>
> How could this technique be adapted for large classes?

5.10 Increased Input & Hidden Input

As we said above, learning is a mysterious business, and students learn in a variety of ways. At least some of them, in our experience, react poorly to overt correction. Dialogues such as this are common:

S I'm going in Scotland.

T To Scotland.

S Yes, to Scotland.

(5 minutes later)

S Are you going in Japan, Keiko?

T To Japan.

S To Japan.

(5 minutes later)

S OK, I'm going in city centre now. Bye!

Leaving aside for a moment the point of whether the preposition is worth correcting, we can see that overt correction is not working. Perhaps the student would respond better to more input on the same point – that is, other activities and exercises which expose them further to the same language item. It is highly likely that they need more correct input (listening and reading) before we can expect correct output!

The problems associated with this are four-fold:

1. remembering the mistakes
2. preparing material specially
3. crowded syllabuses
4. student boredom.

TASK 49

What materials can be used to record students' mistakes during a lesson without disturbing the flow? Think of at least two or three.

Many teachers will say that they do not have the time or the resources to prepare material specially just to deal with students' mistakes – it's much quicker and more economical to just correct them there and then in class. This may be true in the short term: students often manage to put overt correction into practice immediately. But what about the following lesson, and the one after that? If one calculates the number of times a particular student has to be corrected in order to change *in* to *to*, it is hardly an efficient use of the teacher's or student's time over a longer period. In fact, we could turn this on its head – you waste time correcting!

The argument about crowded syllabuses and student boredom both arise with the revision and recycling of material. *We just do not have the time to revisit everything five or six times* is a familiar cry. But all our experience shows that **this** is exactly how a foreign language is learned. In other words, teachers who plead a crowded syllabus are putting teaching before learning. **However much teachers dislike it, teaching less usually involves teaching better.**

However, both problems can be reduced by 'hidden input' – this is input which seems on the surface to do one thing, but also has a secondary purpose – that of revisiting material. In the case of the *in/to* problem, we could propose two possible activities to practise the distinction covertly:

1. Jazz Chant (or similar stress activity):

   Where are you going?

   I'm going to Paris.

   Why are you going?

   I'm going to shop.

   When are you leaving?

   I'm leaving tomorrow.

   etc

2. Alphabet game – each student must repeat the base phrase, adding one more item with the next letter of the alphabet:

   S1 I'm going to London to buy an apple.

   S2 I'm going to London to buy an apple and a bike.

   S3 I'm going to London to buy an apple, a bike and a coat.

   etc.

TASK 50

Prepare hidden input sessions (maximum 10 minutes each) to help students with the following mistakes:

1. I've lived here since six months.
2. She went at home.
3. Who did come to the party?
4. Do you like England?
   – Yes, I like.

5.11 How can I deal with mistakes made during freer activities?

The first question to ask is: do you need to?

TASK 51 _____

> Think of three situations where it is useful for students to know of the mistakes they made during freer activites. What percentage of all freer activities do these constitute?

Obviously, one clear rule which is followed by most teachers is not to interrupt free activities in order to correct. Even the most mistake-obsessed students find this frustrating and annoying. (The only exception might be when a mistake made by all the students is making the activity actually impossible.) There is a three-stage process in the management of mistakes in freer activities. This is:

1. How do I note down the mistake?

2. How do I evaluate the mistake?

3. What do I do with the mistake after the activity is over?

Of these three, evaluation is probably the most difficult. Mistakes of intonation, for example, might seem unimportant when the students are discussing the food in the school canteen, but vital when negotiating a new contract in a business simulation. Often a teacher will evaluate a mistake as 'not worth correcting' – this seems practical and sensible. Any decision is the teacher's, based upon their knowledge of the class, and the aims of the course.

Noting the Mistakes
The first priority is to listen to the students – you have to go round and monitor what the students are actually saying to each other. The mistakes can be noted in various ways: notebook, tape- or video-recorder. Make sure you note down the name of the student who made the mistake, to allow for the possibility of self-correction later.

Task 52

Monitoring is easy in a class of 10. But what about in a class of 35? Who could do the monitoring in place of or as well as the teacher?

What to do with the mistakes

The first question is: do you want or need to do anything with them?

You have to balance the long-term and the short-term good. Part of the answer may be in public relations: it can be an immense confidence-builder for students to know that they will **not** be interrupted, but that they **will** get to see what mistakes they made.

You also have to balance long- and short-term solutions. Some of the increased input and hidden input activities we discussed above may be more appropriate in certain circumstances. The short-term techniques discussed below may be appropriate for some, but not all situations:

1. Hot Cards

These are pieces of paper or card with the student's name on them. During the course of the activity, the teacher notes down important or recurring mistakes on the card. It is then given to the student at the end of the activity, either as a chance for them to self-correct immediately, for work in pairs, or as a reference for the future:

Carmen

1.) X I went yesterday to the sea.
   Adverb order!

2.) Pronunciation
   Sandguich - very guell
   /w/ not /gu/

3.) use a plural verb with
   "people" and "police".

(A nice variation the first time you use the cards is to write the students' names on the back, place the cards face up on a large table, and ask students to find their own.)

2. Invoice Books
These work on the same principle as hot cards, but if you use an invoice book with carbons, you then have a copy to keep for yourself as well. This gives you a list both of individual students' problems, and of the whole class, over time. This profile helps you to plan future lessons. It also gives you a record to show colleagues, parents or students who claim you have too relaxed an approach to mistakes!

3. Recall and Correct
This is a technique of asking individual students to recall points during the activity at which the mistake occurred, and ask the student to say it in a different way. Example:

    T Hermann, can you remember exactly what you said about nuclear power?

    H Yes, I said 'I think it isn't a good idea.'

    T (gestures/expresses doubt)

    H I don't think it's....

    T Yes, that's probably better.

TASK 53

Have you used this technique? Do you find it useful? What practical problems does it bring?

If you have not used it, do you think it would work with your classes?

---

4. Recordings
Play the recording back to the students stopping at points of interest, not just mistakes. Ask for reformulations/corrections from the students.

> **TASK 54**_____
>
> What might be the psychological effects of
> this technique? How would you get around
> them?
> What would you have to make sure of
> before you began (do not forget that not
> everybody likes being taped)?

Alternatively, take the recording away, and note down
the mistakes for further work and/or input.

5. Open 'Remedial' Sessions
All the above techniques require the teacher to focus on
particular, named, students. This might not be a good idea
in some cases – especially if all the mistakes are made by
the same person. One solution is to put the mistakes on the
board or an overhead projector, and ask for reformulations
in pairs, groups or in open class.

5.12 Correcting v Reformulating in natural language

Some teachers believe that language is a 'binary' process: it
is either right or wrong. Others (including us) believe that
language is on a scale from 'What a native-speaker would
say' through 'What a native-speaker might say' to 'What a
native-speaker probably wouldn't say'. As we discussed in
Chapter 1, Michael Lewis has suggested that using a
spectrum of likelihood is likely to be more productive than
the simple right-wrong opposition.

One of the aims of language teaching is to move the
students gradually along the scale. It may be useful, when
using the techniques discussed above, to put the accent on
showing the students how a native-speaker would say a
particular thing, rather than correcting their sentences just
enough to make them acceptable. For example, a student
might say: *I'm not so keen on go to the cinema.*

The temptation is to correct *go* to *going*. But it might be
more profitable to rephrase the whole sentence as a
native-speaker would express the idea. So:

Student: *I am keen on go to the cinema this evening.*

Acceptable: *I am keen on going to the cinema this evening.*

Native-speaker: *I'd really like to go and see a film this evening.*

Again students learn effectively from being exposed to natural language which they understand. If the teacher completes only the first part of the reformulation, the student is left with a sentence which is superficially correct, but which would never actually be uttered.

Task 55

Can you think of problems with such a technique? Here are some students' (spoken) sentences. Think of:

a. An acceptable version of what the student said

b. What a native-speaker would say

1. We succeeded in preventing the flat to be burned.

2. I confused I was still in my dream.

3. My favourite film that I see in the last time is....

4. A holiday can be cheap for a camping goer.

What problems did you have?
Now turn to page 121 for a discussion of these examples.

Teachers of large classes may object that such techniques are impossible for them. Certainly, we do not say that every time a student says something wrong, the teacher must go through what seems a very complicated procedure. It is much more a question of a change of attitude: instead of a teacher thinking *I must correct this mistake* s/he could think *What new and natural language can I provide at this point to help the student?* This is almost certainly more effective in the long term.

CHAPTER 6

WRITTEN ENGLISH – PREPARING AND CHECKING

6.1 **The differences between speaking and writing**

In the previous chapter, we concentrated on two basic 'rules' of how to deal with mistakes in spoken English. These were that

a. comprehensibility, not perfection, is the aim

b. the students should take as much responsibility for their own mistakes as possible.

While these two rules still hold good for writing, there are important differences. These stem from the fact that writing and speaking have different rules themselves, and different things are important. Look at this conversation extract:

A When I saw him the other day, well, it was yesterday, actually, he was looking down.

B What, you mean, at the pavement?

A (shakes head) No, I mean, depressed – he was looking depressed, as if he was still thinking about Lucy.

B Well, he always does.

A Does what?

B Look depressed. He did even before he met Lucy.

This illustrates some of the essential differences between speaking and writing. When speaking, you can modify what you say by repeating, rephrasing, hesitating, starting again, gesturing. You can 'improve' your message by looking angry or encouraging, raising your eyebrows, digging your elbow into the other person's ribs, and so on. As a listener, you can check the message by asking for repetition or clarification, by looking doubtful or puzzled, or, in certain countries, by hand movements. When writing, you do not have these possibilities: your message must be understandable and clear first time.

Furthermore, outside the classroom, written work which has a lot of mistakes, even if these are relatively minor, tends to be frowned upon:

```
                                    16 Godber St
                                    Fishford
                                    Devon
                                    5 Dec 91


Dear Sir

    I wold like to apply for the
job.of secretry to the managing
director.
    please send me details as soon
as possible,

Yours sincerely,
```
Kate Potts
Kate Potts

We can predict the reaction of the recipient of this letter. Perhaps Kate wold have got the job if she had foned? 'Real life' values accuracy in written work highly – depending on the situation, perhaps as highly as intelligibility.

Task 56

Think of three situations in real life where mistakes in written work would be penalized in some way. Are these situations ones where students of the language might be involved?

Finally, most examinations are still based upon the written rather than the spoken word, and although we may not like the fact, students need to be prepared in various writing activities (even though they may never need these skills again after the exam).

There is another point to remember about writing: it is difficult and it is different from speaking. Students who are good at speaking the language will not necessarily be good at writing it, and vice versa. Many people cannot write well in their own language, so they will need even more help and encouragement in a second language.

Task 57

List six writing activities you have given to your students recently. How many of them were designed to consolidate other work, and how many specifically to develop their writing skills?

How many of the activities would be ones that the students might genuinely have to do in 'real life' in English or their own language?

Does it matter? Or can such activities be 'good practice' anyway?

These two factors, that writing requires more correctness and that it is a difficult skill of its own, mean that there are four great dangers into which the teacher can fall:

1. Not preparing students enough.
2. Testing something different from what you think you are testing.
3. Not encouraging students to check their work.
4. Blind correction.

The following discussion of mistakes in writing deals with the first three of these categories. The final point is dealt with in a chapter (chapter 7) of its own.

TASK 58

Think about what you wrote in a foreign language at school. Then answer these questions:

1. What did you write? (poems? newspaper articles?)
2. How was the writing organised?
3. How was the correction done? Who by?
4. By what methods was the correction brought to the students' notice?
5. What is your general feeling about the writing that you did?

6.2 Lack of Preparation

When the authors were at school and university, and learning French, the answers to the above questions were:

1. Compositions, translations and dictations only.
2. We were given a title and a number of words to write.
3. The correction was done by the teacher in red pen.
4. The work was given back with the corrections; the teacher gave us the correct answers and a mark.
5. Our feelings about this system do not bear repeating.

We believe that the situation in EFL is rather better than this, but the tendency is still 'Give out a title – correct every mistake in the composition – give it back and tell the students the answers'.

TASK 59

Is this what happens in your classes? Do you think it is an effective system? If you do, why?

If you do not think it is effective, why do you continue to do it? What alternatives can you think of?

One of the problems is that, once again, there are two types of student: those who like their written work to be as correct as possible, and those who use their written work to 'test the boundaries' of the language. In fact, many students who try to be as correct as possible when speaking in class, will nevertheless be adventurous in their written work. And, once again, it is the teacher's responsibility to help both groups.

Good preparation is one way of doing this. This preparation is at least as helpful as vigorous correction afterwards. Preparation for us means two things:

a. general help with the conventions and rules of written English

b. specific help with the particular activity or exercise the students are going to do.

General help would of course be built into a course of lessons, and would include elements like paragraphing, punctuation, lay-out etc. Many of these are assumed by both teachers and students to be the same from one language to another, and they are the cause of many mistakes. It is outside the scope of this book to provide specific ideas, but there are now a number of writing skills books which will help you.

Specific help with activities (and remember that we are talking about activities designed to improve writing skills, not just consolidate other work) depends enormously on the level and age of the students, their aims and needs, and the constraints of the syllabus.

One procedure often found in language classes is the following:

a. the teacher 'does' the present simple with an elementary class for the first time

b. for homework, s/he asks the students to write a composition entitled 'A day in my life' (maximum 100 words)

Task 60

Do you ask your students to do this? How do you feel about it? Do you do it with a specific aim in mind? What?

The result, more often than not, is a word-for-word translation from the mother-tongue, with a dictionary used for the words which the student did not learn in class. The teacher is then in the position of having to decide between correcting all the mistakes – which may discourage students – and correcting only some things, and feeling guilty that they have not given their students enough feedback.

The advantage of preparing students for the exercise – including doing some of the exercise first – is that they are able to be creative, if they want to be, within a safe framework. The longer the course goes on, the more the element of safety can be reduced. Here we provide two 'guided writing' exercises to illustrate the point.

Write a paragraph, choosing from the alternatives in the boxes. The complete paragraph must make sense.

Last year	, I went to	the USA , with
summer		France
		Africa

my father.	We set off from England on	6th February
my family.		2nd July
some friends.		14 December

and travelled by	plane to	New York , arriving
	boat	Paris
	car	Nairobi

6 hours	later.
11 hours	
a week	

Write long answers to these questions to form a paragraph.

Where do you live?

How far is that from your school?

How do you come to school?

What time do you leave home?

What time do you get to school?

Do you enjoy the journey?

TASK 61

Make a list of the

a. advantages

b. disadvantages

of both these exercises. Do you think the advantages outweigh the disadvantages?

What kinds of students would they be most suitable for?

Have you used these kinds of exercises? What was the result? What, in your experience, do the students feel about them?

Another problem which students are often asked to face without much preparation is collocation – how words fit together in regular patterns. This is the area where vocabulary and grammar overlap. Very often, if a student does not know how to put words together, s/he will have to invent a longer, more grammaticalised way of expressing the idea. The result will often contain grammar mistakes. So, vocabulary problems cause grammar mistakes! If you do not know the expression *a wooden house*, it is reasonable to guess *a house made by wood*. That creates two problems – first there is a mistake, but also, unless the teacher is very careful, it will be corrected to *a house made of wood*, which although the correct version of what the learner wrote, is still not natural English.

This suggests it will be helpful to prepare learners by doing collocation practice **before** asking them to write sentences. The following practice shows one way of preparing students.

Choose a noun which is important for the theme. Ask students to list:

> five **adjectives or nouns** that can come **immediately in front of the key noun** (*book ...exercise book*)

> three **nouns** which can **follow the key noun directly** (*book...bookshop*)

> five **verbs** which can come **in front of the noun** (*book...finish a book*).

Ask students to compare suggestions in pairs and eliminate the least interesting words such as *old, big,* etc. With a larger class, ask two pairs to work in fours and eliminate again. Groups report to whole class; teacher arbitrates on the possible/ impossible collocations suggested and also lists on the board the most useful ones. Students record the most useful ones. This is best done in a shape like this:

Verbs	Adjectives or Nouns	
		(keyword)

We suggest that five adjectives and five verbs are enough for students to record in any one lesson. If you wish to check whether or not a word is useful for this kind of practice, try to think of adjectives and verbs yourself. If you easily think of seven of each, you will find the word useful as a key word for students.

6.3 Testing the Wrong Thing

We have stressed before the individuality of students. Although modern writing materials tend to be better in this respect, it is nevertheless true that when we ask students to write something, we often confuse 'using English' with 'using their imagination' or 'using their knowledge of the world' or something else. We are not saying that students should not use their imaginations and knowledge, just that teachers should be aware of what is going on.

TASK 62

What do the following composition titles test, apart from English?

1. A day in the life of a rock star.

2. The advantages and disadvantages of beards.

3. Capital punishment.

4. Write a composition which begins *'I had never been to a fair before...'*

5. Colours.

6. Write about the differences in your home town between when you were young and now.

We have to remember that some students are not naturally creative or imaginative, and also that many students are studying writing with specific practical aims – report writing, business letter writing, telex writing and so on. So you have to leave a place for both creativity **and** lack of creativity!

TASK 63

Devise three writing activities for an intermediate class which would be suitable for both

a. students who like to be creative and
b. students who are not creative but are nevertheless highly interested in producing good, polished writing.

6.4 Lack of Checking

Writing Together

Writing is often viewed as a lonely business – the poet in the attic room, the examinee sweating over the composition – but in reality, quite a lot of writing is a co-operative matter. (This book, for example.) Books and articles are edited, translations are checked. So why not co-operative writing as part of a language course? Because writing is often used to test students' English, that does not mean writing should **always** be used as a test. Co-operative writing can be more accurate and more imaginative. As such, it is a more valuable part of the language learning process.

While it is convenient to give writing for homework, it may be more sensible, at least at the beginning of a course, to practise it in class. One advantage of writing in groups is that it instils the practice of simultaneous revision and checking which is one of the essences of good writing.

TASK 64

What opportunities do you give for co-operative writing in your classes?

What kinds of writing lend themselves to this?

Which ones are less suitable?

What other advantages does it have apart from the one above?

Checking Together

Research shows that up to 20% of written mistakes can be identified and corrected by the writers themselves. But of course this checking has to be done before the work is handed in.

> **T**ASK **65**
>
> What scope do you give your students for
> **a.** checking each other's work
> **b.** checking their own work
> before handing it in?

6.5 Training Exercises for Checking

One of the most obvious ways of training students to check work is to prepare a copy of the students' work with the mistakes uncorrected, and give them five minutes to find as many mistakes as possible. One problem with this kind of exercise is that the students **know** there is a mistake – it is perhaps more realistic to include some sentences which are correct as well. Below are some activities which combine looking to see if there are mistakes, finding and correcting them.

The students are given a maze with numbers connected by black and white arrows. Below the maze are 15 sentences, some of which are correct and some wrong.

Clear instructions are essential. The students' task is to start at the 'IN' sentence, visit each number once, and arrive at OUT. First they read the IN sentence. If they think it is correct, they follow the white arrow to sentence 3; if they think it is wrong, they follow the black arrow to sentence 14. White is always correct, black is always wrong. In our example, 'IN' is wrong, so the students should go to 14. They then continue in the same way, following the white arrow if a sentence is correct, and the black if it is wrong. The students must also write down the path they followed. One of the advantages of the game is that if they arrive at OUT without visiting all the numbers, they can see – without the teacher telling them – that they have gone wrong somewhere, and must start again.

Mistakes Maze

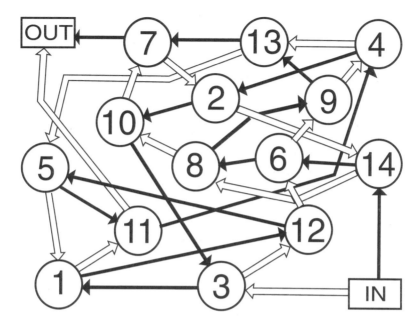

IN I was such tired that I fell asleep.

1. I wish I'd left school at 16 instead of 18.

2. Thanks, but you really should have bothered.

3. Two people were asked to take part in the experiment.

4. If I were you, I'd stay at the Grand Hotel.

5. He apologised for being late.

6. If I'll be away, I'll get someone else to do it.

7. It's the prettiest town I've ever seen.

8. When I was young, I used to playing football in the park.

9. As soon as I left school, I got a job.

10. The 'No Smoking' sign means you don't have to smoke in here.

11. She told me to meet her outside the British Museum.

12. If I find $5 in the street, I'd take it to the police.

13. However he's good at English, he never does his homework.

14. If I didn't miss the bus to the airport, I would have been on the plane which crashed!

To construct a similar game for your students, you can copy the diagram on page 75. All you need to do is make sure that where we have put a correct sentence, you do the same, and where we have put a wrong one, you do the same. Clearly, it can be used at any level, but it must be done in groups to allow for discussion.

Grammar Auction

(This idea comes from Grammar Games by M.Rinvolucri (CUP).)

The game proceeds in exactly the same way as an auction. The students (in groups) have to buy correct sentences, and avoid buying incorrect ones. Each group has £5000 to spend, and they should obviously try to spend as little money as possible. The winning group is the one that has bought the most correct sentences: if two groups have the same number of correct sentences, the group which has spent less money is the winner.

Before the auction begins, the groups should be given enough time to sort through the sentences and decide which are correct. They should also decide how much they want to spend on each sentence.

While the auction is actually proceeding, you should not tell them which are correct. This can be left until afterwards, when the students can also give you the correct version of the wrong sentences. Make sure somebody keeps a record of the auction as it is going on.

If you are constructing a similar auction, make sure that there is a good mix of correct and incorrect examples, and also that in one or two cases, it is not too easy to tell.

Here is an example, suitable for intermediate students.

	Right or Wrong?	Budget
1. Do you have some sugar?	_____	_____
2. I'm very fond of the classical music.	_____	_____
3. She spent £60 for a new dress.	_____	_____
4. Would you like to come round for supper tonight?	_____	_____
5. This is the best fish I've ever had.	_____	_____
6. She works like a waitress in a French restaurant.	_____	_____
7. If I could, I would.	_____	_____
8. Turn it off, would you?	_____	_____
9. The bank in Queen Street has been robbed yesterday.	_____	_____
10. This man worked by my uncle for ten years.	_____	_____

CHAPTER SEVEN

MANAGING WRITTEN MISTAKES

7.1 The Red Pen Syndrome

Many students of a foreign language are asked to write a composition on a difficult subject without help or preparation. The compositions are returned and resemble a battlefield:

... j'ai marché dans le bar et demander pour une bière. À la table dans le coin de la chambre j'ai vu la femme que j'avais déjà vu le jour avant.....

TASK 66

What are the effects of this kind of correcting?

Apart from the pyschological effects of this correcting, many of the things we said in the introduction should be repeated here:

1. Don't expect perfection. Concentrate on where the students' writing is effective, as well as where it is defective.

2. Mistakes are often a sign of learning.

3. Mistakes come and go – a student's 'correctness' goes up and down from day to day.

4. Good writing, like all language learning, is a long-term process.

5. Some mistakes are more important than others.

TASK 67

Put the following mistakes in order of importance for three different students:

a. a 19-year-old who is learning general English

b. a business person learning to write reports for their US parent company

c. a student preparing for the writing part of an exam such as Cambridge First Certificate

Here are the mistakes:

1. A spelling mistake for example, *sanwich* for *sandwich*.

2. A long and partially incomprehensible sentence: *There is nothing that they have to consider when the cleaner is coming, when the meal is prepared or what is preparing or what else.*

3. A grammar mistake where comprehension is not affected: *Next year, I am thinking to go to the US.*

4. A conjunction at the start of a paragraph which leaves the reader confused and perplexed.

5. A repeated vocabulary mistake: *plays* described as *comedies* four or five times in one piece.

6. An 'elementary' grammar mistake sometimes wrong, sometimes correct in the same piece.

7. A mistake of register, for example a word which is too informal:
I screwed up instead of *I made a mistake.*

8. No paragraphs

9. A mistake where the meaning is not clear: *If a man attacks you, you must kick him in the kidnaps.*

10. A punctuation mistake where comprehension is not affected: *She arrived on monday.*

7.2 Reacting to Content

When students give you a piece of written work, you generally have time to look at it in detail: you can use this time to show the student different reactions to different aspects of the work. Generally speaking, it is important to be encouraging even when – or especially when – the student's work is weak overall.

It is rare for a piece of work not to have several parts which are good, correct, interesting and deserving of positive comment. These must be acknowledged. Students must get to know what is good as well as what is 'wrong'.

Furthermore, we can react to the content in a way that is not always possible in class. There is much to be said for interesting work containing mistakes, rather than 'perfect' but dull, safe, writing. This also needs to be encouraged – especially if you have given a writing assignment where creativity is one of the aims. (Even from a practical point of view, creativity is useful: examiners tend to favour interesting writing, which often 'hides' mistakes.)

TASK 68

When giving back written work, what room do you leave for

a. praising accurate work?

b. praising interesting/creative work?

7.3 Restrictive Correcting

Many written assignments are given to students in order to consolidate work done in class. In these cases, the teacher often feels justified in concentrating on the mistakes which concern the language point in question, and ignoring the others. As a way of reducing the volume of correcting, this technique can also be extended to other kinds of written work. One week, a teacher might decide to work only on mistakes with prepositions, say, or spelling, or tenses.

TASK 69

What are the advantages and disadvantages of such an approach? How do you think students would react to it? What difference would it make if the students are, or are not, told before they do the work that this approach will be used?

7.4 Involving Students

The following is a fairly typical piece of correction of written work:

*The price of petrol is **GOING** getting up and a lot of people **ARE !!** is worried about the effect on*

TASK 70

Bearing in mind what we said about the correction of oral mistakes in chapters 3 and 4, what disadvantages can you see with this method of correcting?

We would certainly recommend the active involvement of students in the process of dealing with mistakes, for three reasons:

1. Active, involved students learn better. Just accepting corrections given by the teacher is unlikely, even in the short term, to bear much fruit. The student is more likely to put away the book and shrug their shoulders. An active process of mistakes management engages the

student intellectually and is therefore likely to be more effective.

2. It induces a more co-operative atmosphere in class. Certain students accept and learn from self-correction and correction by other students much more readily than from the teacher.

3. Less focus on the teacher. As we pointed out in the introduction, we are trying to make the students more independent. It seems unlikely that a correction process where the students are helpless 'victims' of the teacher's red pen will have this effect.

TASK 71 _____

> Do you agree? The above is opinion, not fact.
> What does your experience tell you? Have you taught students for whom this kind of student independence has been unsuitable? Why?

Once again, we would point out that some students feel a strong resistance to the teacher taking a back seat when it comes to the correction of their written work. (In fact, it would be true to say that 99% of students, even those who enjoy and see the value of self- and peer-correction, like to have the final decision, the final judgment, made by the teacher.) Why bother to ask another student when the teacher is available? The answer is, of course, that the teacher may be available now, but won't be for ever. But this needs to be explained to the students.

7.5 Active Mistake Management
Warning: as we saw in the previous chapter, there are many factors to consider when deciding what and how much to correct in students' work. It may be unwise to correct all the mistakes. In some of the following examples, however, for the sake of economy of space and clarity, all the mistakes have been noted or corrected.

1. Self-correction without indication of mistakes
Read through each student's work, noting down the mistakes made:

The work is then given back and the students read through their work individually, and find and correct the mistakes. You might set a time limit, or allow as much time as they like. Then you might take in the work to see how successful they have been.

2. Peer-correction
The same as the above, but with the students working in pairs on their partner's script. This is undoubtedly more effective, as students, like anybody else, find it easier to see other people's mistakes than their own.

3. Underlining Mistakes
Indicate mistakes by underlining:

The students then try and correct their mistakes. Again, they are encouraged to work in pairs and groups, which gives them the chance to discuss the best alternative, in English or their own language. In this way, the discussion helps learning, even if not all the mistakes are corrected.

4. Mistakes Underlined and Coded

You not only indicate **where** the mistake is, but also what **type** of mistake it is by using a correcting code. Here is one possible correcting code:

GR	= grammar	**( )**	= unnecessary word(s)
W.O.	= word order	**P**	= punctuation
T	= tense	**reg**	= register
VOC	= vocabulary	**?**	= don't understand
SP	= spelling	**⋏**	= word missing
A	= article	**!**	= careless mistake

TASK 72

Have you used a code like this? Have you found it useful? What are its advantages and disadvantages? What changes would you make?

This, of course, is only one possible code. Every teacher needs to develop a personal one. Some teachers, for example, prefer to give symbols for various kinds of grammatical mistake. This might happen especially if the class is working on a particular grammatical point. So, instead of **GR**, we could use **c/uc** for a problem with countable and uncountable nouns.

One aspect of the code above is that it does not give much scope for providing encouragement and praise. After all, feedback on 'correct' work is just as important as feedback on 'wrong' or 'ineffective' work – how much longer we remember good work we have done than poor work! Obviously, writing *Good* or *Very Good* in the margin is an option, but there are certainly plenty of other ways of doing it.

TASK 73

Devise three different ways – using symbols – of praising good work, two for adults and one for children.

It is important, however, to be as informative about good work as about 'wrong' work. If you just write *Good* at the side, the student does not know if it means 'correct', 'interesting idea' or 'well-chosen vocabulary' and so on.

TASK 74

A correcting code such as the one above depends on the mistake being clearly categorisable. But look at the following 5 mistakes – which category would you put them in?

1. We didn't go to the beach, however it was a nice day.

2. It was raining, but I fell happy.

3. I yearn for England as a young boy.

4. Spanish women I know are good drivers.

5. Maria doesn't have the eyes blue like me.

What steps are available to us when the root of the mistake is unclear? What do you do? Does it really matter?

Two final, important, points about the correcting code:

a. Consistency and unambiguity are important. Once you have used a set of symbols, you should keep to them. You should always use the same symbol for the same kind of mistake, and only for that.

b. You must familarise the students with the code from the start. Ask the students to write it down somewhere permanently, so they can always refer to it.

Please turn to p116 for practice compositions to correct, using a correcting code.

5. Search and Correct

You indicate there is a mistake by putting either an X or a code symbol in the margin of the line where the mistake is. The students, knowing which line it is in, look for it and try and correct it.

> x Last Sunday we drived from my house to
> x the mauntains. Because it was a very
> xx long travel, we have started early, about
> xx at 6 o'clock a.m.

> voc.   Last Sunday we drived from my house to
> sp.   the mauntains. Because it was a very
> voc.+t. long travel, we have started early, about
> w.o.+() at 6 o'clock a.m.

Clearly, the technique with the code symbols makes the students' job easier and also less likely that they will change material that was already correct.

6. Mistakes Referred to a Grammar or Textbook

Underline the mistakes and number them according to pages or paragraphs of a grammar or textbook which all the students can refer to. Students can then look up anything they cannot correct or are not sure about.

> **496/502**
>
> I'm working in a bank now for about three years. I must say it <u>203</u> is a bit boring, but it is <u>enough well-paid</u> for me to live comfortably.

In the above example, the numbers refer to paragraphs in *Practical English Usage, Michael Swan, Oxford University Press.*

7. Hot Cards and Invoice Books

As we saw with spoken mistakes in chapter 5, hot cards are a useful way of getting students to focus their attention on the mistakes they make most often. Hot cards can also be used with written mistakes. However, rather than giving each student a hot card with each piece of work handed back, it is a better idea to use hot cards as a record of the mistakes which have recurred most for each student in two or three pieces of writing. This gives the students a clearer idea of the mistakes which they keep making.

It is a good idea, when using hot cards, to write in a small invoice book with carbon papers. Write the student's name on his/her individual hot card, give out the hot cards, and keep the carbon copies in the invoice book. This, with the name of the class written on it, can now be used as a reliable permanent record of the recurrent mistakes of individual students and of the class as a whole. This permanent record is very useful for helping the teacher to plan future lessons.

TASK 75

Of the seven ideas above, how many have you used?

Which have been the most and the least useful?

What other correction schemes have you used?

7.6 Peer-Correction in Large Classes

Many teachers feel that, with their large classes, correction by the students is impractical. Not true! Correction in pairs and groups is still possible, as can be seen in the following diagram:

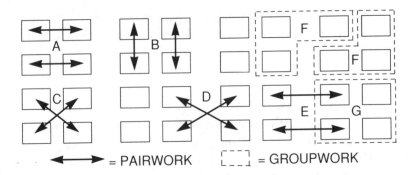

← → = PAIRWORK   ⌐ ⌐ = GROUPWORK

The letters in the diagram show that there are many different possible combinations for pairwork (A, B, C, D, E) and groupwork (F, G). A word of warning: when putting the class into pairs or groups like this, particularly when it is new to them, it is essential to give clear, precise instructions. All the students must know exactly what they have to do and who they have to work with. Unclear instructions sometimes produce chaos, and chaos can lead to discouragement. Make sure you check that the students know what to do – perhaps by asking them to repeat it back to you. A board diagram can help.

These kinds of activities need to be prepared. Make sure, too, that you vary the groups and pairs, and avoid always putting the same students together.

TASK 76 _____

> If you have a large class, what is your reaction to the above? Can you see objections to it?
>
> What other ways of organising peer-correction can you think of?

7.7 The Inadequacy of 'local' correction

As we have mentioned above, there are numerous differences between written and spoken language. One that we have not mentioned is this: written language tends to be an ordered sequence of ideas, with a logical progression. Since the reader cannot check or ask for repetition, the relationship between parts of the text must be as clear as possible.

This leads us to make a distinction between 'global' and 'local' mistakes. Often, we find, even when we have corrected the piece of work in one of the ways suggested above, the student is not left with a piece of 'real' English. And vice versa: some students produce work which, whilst having numerous individual mistakes, nevertheless reads well as a whole.

Global mistakes are likely to be found at a level which is larger than the sentence. At the lowest level, this might be a mistake in the connections between the sentences. Taken on its own, the following would pass unnoticed:

> *Despite this, Ford has made great progress in the UK market.*

until it follows this:

> *Ford have always targeted the UK as a potential growth area for its products.*

However, in a sense, this is just another 'local' mistake. Genuinely global mistakes are at the level of the paragraph or the complete piece. Often, the 'mistakes' in the piece do not lend themselves to correction of the kind which were considered suitable for individual mistakes. How, then, can we deal with them?

7.8 Feeding Back

We said in chapter 5 that often the student would like to know how a native-speaker would say a particular thing, rather than just have the correction of what they have written. (And it is a good idea to prepare students for writing by showing them plenty of examples of native-speaker writing.) Furthermore, mistake-management must help the students constructively, not just judge or criticise. It seems likely that the quality of the feed-back from the teacher is one of the crucial factors in the development of writing skills.

One way of feeding back is through reformulation. Look at the following letter, produced by an intermediate student:

Dear Madame and Sir,

I've just seen your advertisements about your package holidays. I'm looking forward to do such a journey, and I have some questions for you. Specially the price is an important point for me, because I am a student. I want to go two weeks to Sri Lanka. Are there special dates you arrange this kind of holiday or is that variable?

Besides I would be interested in Pakistan, but aren't there now any flights? I think it is a little bit dangerous to do some holidays there. Unless I am wrong, please send me the price for two weeks and the date too.

If the dates are not variable, could you arrange a two-week holiday in a place like the two others between 1st June and 14th June.

Please answer me as soon as possible.

We see that, although it is quite comprehensible, it sounds unnatural for two main reasons:

a. register

b. sentence and paragraph construction.

As many teachers know from experience, this kind of loose-jointed writing is quite common even at more advanced levels. A recent study has shown that 29% of all written grammatical mistakes are due to the students having a faulty concept of what constitutes a correct sentence.*

` In these cases, going through and correcting every individual mistake (assuming we could identify them) may be less helpful than showing the student how a native-speaker would express these ideas more naturally. This means reconstructing individual sentences, or reformulating the whole piece of work.** The student can then compare this reconstructed/reformulated version with the original.

TASK 77

Try reformulating the above letter. What differences can you see between your version and the original? How would you present them to the student?

7.9 Correcting for Examinations

Many of the ideas in this book are based on the idea that language-learning is a long-term process. Unfortunately, many of our students are studying for written examinations: not only is the preparation time limited, but also the exams themselves often reward accuracy, many of them overtly stating that the successful students will avoid mistakes.

On the face of it, this means that a teacher who is preparing students for such an exam will spend a long time correcting students' written work, and trying to eliminate mistakes. We are not suggesting that a responsible teacher should necessarily abandon this approach, but we do feel that many of the principles behind mistake management are still valid on even the shortest of exam courses:

1. The students must be involved in the process – the corrections should not always come from the teacher, but from the students as well.

* ELTJ vol 49/1 Jan'89 'How to cope with Spaghetti Writing' – Damien McDevitt

** See ELTJ vol 42/2 April'88 'Mistake correction' – Keith Johnson

2. Students must be well-prepared for the tasks they are asked to do.

3. Students should be encouraged to work together on accuracy – checking each other's work, for example.

4. Not all of the lesson, or all of the course, should be devoted to accuracy – even in the strictest exam course, there is room for experimentation and imagination.

5. Students must be encouraged at all times.

7.10 A Final Point

Some years ago, a colleague was correcting a composition and underlined a sentence she thought sounded rather unnatural. The student came up to her after she had handed it back and said: 'Actually that was the only sentence I didn't write: that was written by Oscar Wilde!'

Any reaction by teachers to a piece of written work by their students has to run a fine line between letting students break the rules, and telling them when they do. Any creative writing does break the rules. On the other hand, breaking the rules means knowing what the rules are, and a lot of writing by foreign students is a conscious testing-out of the rules. Even elementary students do this: trying out bits and pieces from various sources, from pop songs, from films they have seen, from advertisements, and so on, to see if it works. Sometimes it does, sometimes it does not. Students must not be discouraged from experimenting – but they must be allowed to know the results of their experiments.

Language learning is not only, or even mostly, about knowing and applying rules. It is, as Christopher Candlin has pointed out, about forming hypotheses, and testing them. This sounds impressive, but in practice it frequently means a student thinking or guessing that two things are similar or different, and producing a sentence based on the hypothesis. If the sentence 'works' – this might mean the student gets what he or she wants, or, in the classroom, the teacher approves the sentence – the student's hypothesis is strengthened, and a small step is made in the learning process. On the other hand, if the sentence does not 'work', the student gets evidence that the hypothesis was false.

Stephen Krashen has pointed out that some language learners are good observers of the evidence they get back, while others are not. He claims that students really master language through forming a hypothesis, experimenting, and then 'monitoring' their own output, and the reaction it gets. He claims that the most effective learners will be those who are what he calls 'optimal monitor users'.

These two linguists, in their different ways, both want us to encourage students to hypothesize, and to experiment. They claim that this process **is** the process of language learning.

On a more personal, or psychological, level, Michael Lewis has pointed out that whatever teachers think they are doing, the fact is that you never correct a mistake, you always correct a person.

The ideal is that students learn to monitor their own output, and the feedback they get. The teacher provides an important element of this feedback. What is important, however, is that the feedback is positive in its overall effect – if it discourages or depresses the student, it may be counter-productive. The purpose of teacher feedback should be to have a long-term positive effect on the students' ability to monitor his or her own output.

As far as writing is concerned, the key to this is communication: before, during and after the writing process. We need to talk to and prepare the students **before** they start writing. We need to give students help and support **during** the writing process – it is often the feeling of isolation which makes writing into a frustrating and demotivating experience. And **after** they have finished writing, we need to give as much useful and constructive feedback as we can: first, we need to talk to the students to discover what they were trying to do, and we must help them to discover if their efforts were successful.

Unfortunately, time does not always allow us the chance to communicate in this way. It is not always possible to ask 30 different students what their aims were in a particular piece of written work! However, we can be sure that time spent in this way will not be wasted.

CHAPTER EIGHT

REMEDIAL WORK

It is a strange fact of life that, although we may see the same thing happen day after day, we still refuse to believe it.

This is especially true if it goes against our established view of the world in some way. This is true as much of language teaching as of any other field. Think about these cries of rage from teachers:

> 'Why do they always miss off the third person -s? There's only one verb change in the present – it's so easy!'

> 'They only learnt that last Friday! How can they have forgotten it already?'

> 'Don't you remember these words from last lesson?'

> 'He's been learning English for a year, and he can hardly say his own name!'

> 'Can you believe it! Studying for Proficiency and she puts "He have"!'

We do not really believe in this chapter. There is no such thing as remedial work.

TASK 78

Is this true, in your opinion? Why? Why not?

Every teacher knows the feeling of frustration which comes from teaching a particular language point, and in the very next lesson the students make mistakes with the same point.

In fact, this happens so often that we could formulate a rule: It is rare for students to understand and use new language immediately. Acquiring language for fluent, accurate and creative use takes a long time. It is an extended process, and instant success is not possible. If the students get something 'wrong', teachers often believe it is because they have not learnt it properly. On one level, this is true. On another level, we are really talking about students' temporary inability to activate fully and accurately language they have met. Learning takes longer than we want to believe. There are several explanations for this:

memory limitations

inappropriate materials

poor learning atmosphere

lack of motivation

TASK 79

Can you add to this list?

8.1 Remedial vs Revisiting

The word 'remedial' suggests failure. It suggests that students who cannot put language to use immediately need special treatment. This is not usually true: they need the same treatment, just more of it.

We have said many times that students vary enormously. But language varies enormously, too, especially in its 'learnability' and this learnability varies from person to person.

TASK 80 _____

Try this simple test. Below are ten words from a foreign language, with their English meanings.

Spend a few minutes studying them, then leave them for an hour or two. Then write down as many of the ten words as possible with their English translations. Then try and analyse why some of them were easier for you than others.

takkel – door key (vb)   **gimsen** – pronounce

flignet – shepherd   **wahmet** – light switch

orn – bird   **dimmenauswach –** inflation

lastnen – divorce (vb)   **blooed** – rich

grompy – grumpy   **engorgung** – blockage

In the field of vocabulary, where memory is particularly important, it is clear that some words are easier to remember than others: perhaps because they relate more to our special field of interest, perhaps because they are similar to a word in our own language, or simply because they are vivid in some way to us. A Spanish-speaker will find the word *important* easier to remember than an Arabic speaker; a doctor may recall *stethoscope* rather than *screwdriver*. But even in the area of grammar, some 'rules' seem easier to absorb than others: students seem to recall the present perfect continuous surprisingly easily (considering how 'difficult' it is supposed to be) whereas they more commonly miss out the auxiliary from the present continuous.

TASK 81

> Think of a foreign language you know well
> (English, if you are a non-native speaker).
> Make a list of
> **a.** vocabulary
> **b.** grammatical points
> you have found both particularly easy and
> particularly hard to 'learn'. If you can,
> compare notes with another person in the
> same situation: do your lists agree?

The clear implication is that everything must be re-taught and re-visited, not just the elements which come up as 'mistakes' in class. All language learning is based on continual exposure, hypothesizing and, even with the correct hypotheses, testing and reinforcing the ideas behind them.

8.2 Remedial Teaching within school systems

Actually, remedial teaching does exist, if only in the minds of school administrators. Any student who fails an end-of-course exam, and is asked to resit, is a remedial student. It is highly improbable that they have learnt nothing during the year: just that they have not learnt fast enough to keep up with the school system. Everybody learns at different speeds: but it is an unusual school which can take this fact fully into account. For this reason, we have 'remedial' classes.

TASK 82

> Have you ever taught a so-called 'remedial'
> class? What were its main characteristics?

For obvious reasons, the members of a remedial class are very sensitive to failure. Motivating the students to try again is, therefore, of the greatest importance. This can be done by a combination of sensitivity and patience on the part of the teacher and a freshness of approach.

8.3 How can I change my approach?

Presenting the students with the same material, from the same textbook, in the same way, is almost sure to end in 'failure' again. The least the teacher can do is to change the textbook. Ideally, the new one should be based upon different principles from the original one – if a structural course (one where grammatical points decide the ordering of the material for presentation) has not produced the hoped-for results, we may consider using material organised in a non-structural way. These courses tend to stress the immediate use of the new language, and in that sense give the students a visible sign of progress and achievement. Also, an approach where the student is not obliged to produce language which is correct, but rather where the teacher **waits for students to produce language voluntarily**, which is then responded to in a positive way (even if it may not be totally 'correct'), in other words where the aims and ideals are based on longer-term objectives than normal, may produce a better result.

8.4 More Radical Approaches to Remedial Work

As we said at the start of this book, every language learner is an individual, and learns in an individual way. But they are often not taught as individuals. For example, in most classes, all the students. . .

> . . . sit down to learn the lesson;
> . . . use the same coursebook;
> . . . are asked to learn the same language points;
> . . . have little control over what they learn;
> . . . learn the lesson in the same room (usually indoors, usually in lines or in a horseshoe, usually under artificial light, usually with nothing going on in the background, usually inside a 'school').

Since the conventional methods might be said to have failed the students, perhaps radical solutions are required?

TASK 83

What might these solutions be?
Could at least some of these solutions influence your teaching now?

CHAPTER NINE

THE NON-NATIVE SPEAKER

TASK 84

If you are a non-native teacher, answer the following questions:

1. How many of your students' mistakes do you think you notice?
   a. all
   b. most
   c. quite a lot
   d. relatively few

2. Do you think it is important that you notice as many mistakes as possible?

3. Do you think it is important that you correct mistakes after you have noticed them?

4. If you correct a student's mistake, are you always sure that it was really wrong?

5. Was your English corrected a lot when you were a student?

6. If you answered 'Yes', do you think it helped you? Are you sure? Have you any evidence that you couldn't have learned at least as quickly without so much correction?

Non-native speaking teachers of English greatly outnumber the native speakers. If you belong to this majority you will be very aware that you are in a different situation from your native speaking colleagues. This situation leads to special worries and pressures, and these, in our experience, can produce a very particular attitude towards mistakes and correction.

TASK 85

Non-native teachers usually have a number of things in common. How many of the following statements are true for you?

1. You worry about your own English.

2. You live in a culture where the written word has higher prestige than the spoken word.

3. You work within the State school system in your country.

4. Your students take regular, written, examinations.

5. Your teaching involves much more than simply imparting knowledge or 'teaching English' to a group of students (ie you are also involved in the social and personal development of your students).

9.1 Your own language

Native speakers never worry about their own English, and their students never question it. In your case you may worry about your English, and it may, on occasions, be questioned by more advanced students.

From time to time, you will have doubts about whether a particular expression is, or is not, possible in English. It is important for you to realise that this is quite normal. Many native speakers – including some who are teachers – are not very linguistically sensitive. They may be 'sure' that something is or is not possible, but it doesn't always follow that they are right! It is also important to realise that because you have not met a particular expression, it doesn't always mean that it doesn't exist. All teachers, native and non-native, need to keep an open mind about what is possible, and not worry too much about their own language.

It is often counter-productive to concentrate too much on the mistakes of others (in your case, your students'). Sometimes, as we described above, the teacher sees it as her/his job to look for mistakes much or all of the time. And with this idea may come the desire to show people that they have seen the mistake . . . and that means an automatic correction. This reaction is understandable, but may not be helpful to your students.

TASK 86

As a non-native teacher, which of these reactions do you have when you hear either a student or a colleague make a mistake in English (be honest!):

1. Despair ('Oh no, not another one!')

2. Self-satisfaction ('Ha! That's an interesting mistake! I was studying that point just last week.')

3. Relief ('Phew! I spotted that one.')

4. Anticipation ('Another chance to correct...')

5. Envy ('Maybe she makes mistakes occasionally, but I wish I could speak English as fluently as she does!')

6. Something else (write it here):

_____

As a non-native speaker, your English is probably different from a native speaker in two important ways. Firstly, you have less access on a day to day basis to natural English. Of course, you may have opportunities to read English books and newspapers, or to hear radio programmes and even take part in informal conversations – but not on a 24-hours-a-day-7-days-a-week basis. Inevitably you are at something of a disadvantage over the vast range of what is possible and what is not. Secondly, you are much more likely than a native speaker to be influenced by the things you learned yourself when you were a student, and in particular by grammar rules which you learned a long (in some cases a **very** long) time ago!

There are two important things for you to bear in mind here. Firstly, a great many things are possible in language which you may not have heard. We suggest that rather than correcting or worrying about everything that seems new to you, you should adopt a basically tolerant attitude to the language your students produce. Instead of asking 'Is it right?', you can frequently ask 'Can I understand it?'. If you can understand it, we suggest that you look on it positively and favourably, and encourage the students. If you can't understand it, then clearly you have to ask the student about it, or if it is written work, make some written query or correction.

Secondly, it is important to remember that many of the grammar 'rules' which you learned at school, or even at university, are **partial** rules. A comprehensive grammar of English is much larger than most pedagogic grammars. However useful it might be to teach the '*some* in positives, *any* in negatives and questions' rule, it is certainly nowhere near the truth of how English actually works. It is very important for you to realise that if you start applying rules, you will start to correct and worry about many things which are correct and natural already!

You will see that this second suggestion is very much in line with the first – we encourage you to be tolerant towards language, rather than looking for difficulties, problems, and things to correct.

9.2 Your attitude to written and spoken language

TASK 87

Before you read this section, answer these questions:

1. Do you work in a system which values accuracy in written English?
2. Which do you find more serious – written or spoken mistakes?
3. Which do you find it easier to notice – mistakes in your students' spoken English or in their writing?
4. Which mistakes do you correct in your students' written work:
   a. all
   b. most
   c. the most important ones
   d. very few
5. How do you make your overall assessment of your students' English:
   a. on the basis of their writing
   b. on the basis of their speech
   c. using both the students' spoken and written language

You will see from the previous section that we are basically encouraging you to rely on your intuitions, and to use comprehensibility, rather than accuracy, as a way of judging your students' work. This does not mean that accuracy does not matter, but it means there are many other factors to consider as well.

Most non-native teachers working within a State education system are concerned with both written and spoken language. The relative importance placed on the different skills varies from country to country, depending on the syllabus. You may be required to place greater emphasis on reading and writing than on speaking and listening.

Native speakers, on the other hand, are usually employed in situations where speaking and listening are more important, and where oral language is more important than written.

Attitudes towards mistakes in written and spoken language vary. In most cultures, writing is connected with the emotive concept of literacy and 'education'. Most people tend to be less tolerant of mistakes in writing. We expect writing to be careful, thoughtful and, as a result, more accurate. The danger is that, since most teachers would agree that it is easier to notice written mistakes, it becomes tempting to leap in and correct them too. This may not be sufficient reason; and it certainly does not justify **over-** correcting students' written work.

There is a further danger here for the non-native speaker. You may be over-influenced by the fact that you are preparing students for a written examination. This is, of course, important, and means that you need to take serious account of that. But it does not mean **all** your lessons, and **all** of your teaching, need to be conducted as if **everything** that the students say or do is part of that written examination.

9.3 Teaching is more than teaching the language

It is most important for you to realise that your self-esteem, and professional competence, depend on a great deal more than the quality of your own English, and your ability to correct students' mistakes.

Modern teacher training and teacher development courses suggest that teachers have a whole range of professional skills. Which of the following do you recognise yourself doing fairly frequently in class:

Social organiser	Time keeper
Encourager	Counsellor
Language arbiter	Educator
Developing inter-personal skills	Developing exam skills

This list can easily be extended further. The good teacher has to work with colleagues, prepare materials, advise parents, develop students socially, help students discriminate what is and what is not worth learning, and so on.

TASK 88

Make a pie chart such as this one:

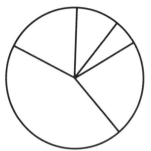

Label the parts of the pie chart according to how you spend your time – for example, if you spend 50% of your time in meetings, divide the pie in half and label it accordingly.

Of course, two important parts of the teacher's job are to know English well, and to help students when they get it wrong. But those are **part** of the job, and if they are taken to extremes, they contradict other important parts of the job – such as encouraging the students, and developing the ability to use language well and imaginatively. It is a matter of balance: the absolute accuracy and correctness of your students' English is probably not the only, or even the main target of your professional skills. Non-native teachers need a wider concept of their self-image so that they do not feel guilty about not correcting every mistake.

It would be very convenient if there was a theory to which we could turn which would tell us when to correct, what to correct and how to correct. This does not exist. What is clear from observing teachers in classrooms is that it is **their own attitude to correction which is the single most important factor which influences their classes**. It is **not** clear that the teachers who correct most are the most successful teachers; there is some evidence that the opposite may be true!

9.4 Your attitude to mistakes

If you take a relaxed attitude to mistakes, your view may be challenged by your students, colleagues, headmaster or the parents. What are you to say to them if this happens? Here, we make some concrete suggestions.

When your students demand to have all their mistakes corrected

1. During one lesson, particularly when your students are talking about something which interests them, stop at every mistake. Do not continue until you have dealt with each one thoroughly. Ask the students at the end of the lesson if they still think it was a good idea.

2. Ask students how they think they will personally improve when you correct mistakes made by other students. Encourage them to see that a lot of time can be wasted by correcting one person when lots of other people don't need the information anyway.

3. Talk to students about how they learned their mother tongue. If students have younger brothers and sisters, ask them to listen to the way they learned their first language. Discuss the matter carefully and calmly. Encourage students to see that making mistakes while learning a language is natural – whether it is your mother tongue or English.

When your colleagues suggest you are irresponsible if you do not correct every mistake

4. Ask them to read this chapter! (with an open mind).

5. Challenge them to produce concrete evidence that correction leads to improvement.

6. Point out that making mistakes is an essential part of mother tongue learning, and of all learning.

If your headmaster challenges your competence

7. Point out that language learning involves making mistakes – it is a natural part of the process.

8. Point out that students gain confidence if they have a sense of achievement, rather than a constant sense of failure.

9. If your headmaster is not a trained English teacher, point out that this book, which has been prepared by competent people in the field, has encouraged you in your view, and it is a view held by many competent trained language teachers worldwide.

When parents question your attitudes

10. Explain how language learning has changed and developed since they were at school. Point out the educational advantages of doing less correction.

11. Tell them that mistakes are not 'wrong English' – they are attempts at correct English. If a student says *'She work in a big office block'*, there are seven words in the sentence, and six of them are correct. It doesn't seem completely reasonable to concentrate only on the bit which is 'nearly right' rather than completely right. Students need to be encouraged for what they get correct, not discouraged by what they get 'wrong'.

12. Above all, point out that there is no direct evidence that correction helps. It is a commonly held 'belief', but many commonly held beliefs are not in fact true!

9.5 Marking

The question of dealing with mistakes becomes particularly important when you have to mark and grade students' work. The most common method used by language teachers is to deduct marks for mistakes. This means students are penalised for what they get wrong, not rewarded for what they get right. Teachers' discussions tend to focus on the grading of mistakes and relative penalties. Perhaps a more positive approach would be desirable.

1. What is the agreed system of marking in your school? Are you happy with it?

2. What problems arise as a result of it?

3. Does it penalise failure or reward achievement?

TASK 89

Devise or research a marking scheme where good work is rewarded, rather than one in which mistakes are penalised. Think about how you could allocate marks for the following: fluency, imagination, creative use of language, making intelligent guesses about the language, good vocabulary, good collocations.

How could you make this marking system as objective as possible, rather than just a subjective impression?

Then look at p122 for some ideas.

A book such as this cannot revolutionise your education system, but it can help your attitudes. If you do mark students' written work, try to put into practice some of the advice in Chapter 7. Above all, whenever you write comments on students' work, try to be encouraging.

9.6 Conclusion

Remember that the best speakers of English are not always the best teachers of English!

Be realistic and honest with your students about your own English. No-one expects a chemistry teacher to hold the Nobel prize for chemistry!

Your worth and value as a teacher are not based only on your language ability. Of equal, if not more, importance, is your expertise at organising your students' learning, and your constant professional search for new and better classroom techniques and methods. Above all, your ability as a teacher depends upon your personal skills of encouragement and motivation.

CHAPTER TEN

CONCLUSION

When the authors started teaching, methodology based on 'behaviourism' was in fashion. One of its principles was that you learned by certain kinds of repetition and imitation: a mistake was a sign of failure, and was corrected immediately; lessons were organised so that mistakes were avoided. In fact, if the students made a lot of mistakes, this was a sign of poor preparation on the part of the teacher.

'Behaviourism' also believed that, since you imitated what you heard, it was bad practice to have too many mistakes around, in case the students imitated them. Exercises like drills or guided writing were designed so that, as far as possible, the student was always writing or speaking only correct English.

As time went on, this view of language learning began to be questioned, and the position of the mistake changed too. If, as some theorists were beginning to believe, learning a language involved testing out hypotheses about a system, finding out if they were right or wrong, and then adjusting the hypothesis accordingly, it became clear that often these hypotheses would be wrong. The emphasis shifted from controlling what students say, to liberating them to say what they like, in order for them to find out for themselves the limits of correctness. Later theory also suggests that hearing imperfect sentences does not lead to a student saying them, so we need not fear students hearing each others' imperfect language. Indeed Stephen Krashen has even suggested students may learn particularly effectively from the language of their fellow students, even if it contains mistakes (because it is at about the right level for students to **understand** and process what they hear).

Of course, students learned under both 'systems' – but teachers have become rather confused, especially about mistakes. It affects their professional pride to hear a mistake go by uncorrected, but on the other hand they know they must not always be the students' safety net.

Let us put this dilemma into practical terms. Here are two typical writing exercises.

Write long answers to these questions, so as to make a short composition:

What's your name?

How old are you?

Where do you live?

How many brothers and sisters have you got?

What do your mother and father do?

Where do you study English?

What do you think of English?

Write a few sentences about yourself and your family.

What would be the result if these two exercises – which are designed to produce more or less the same answer – were given to an elementary class?

We can predict that the students who do the first exercise will produce a composition of seven or eight sentences, most of which will be grammatically (and presumably factually) correct. We can also predict almost exactly what the sentences will be:

> *My name is Fukima. I am 18. I live in Osaka.*
> *I have got one brother and two sisters....*

The students who do the second exercise, on the other hand, will produce work which, depending on the individual student, will have a greater range of inventiveness. It will almost certainly also include a larger number of mistakes. For example, they may decide they want to describe their parents' characters, and so say something like:

My father is a sportive man, and my mother is much sweet.

These mistakes may occasionally lead the composition to be incomprehensible: does *sportive* mean 'active' or 'doing lots of sport' or maybe 'snappy' or even 'cheeky'?

Both these exercises are valid for different reasons. The first practises language already learnt, gives students confidence, and provides them with a correct model for future use. The second gives the students a chance to 'spread their wings', to try out new vocabulary or structures, and, above all, to express themselves.

In other words, the teacher cannot have it both ways. You cannot ask students to be both linguistically creative and completely accurate: the two things are, by the nature of language learning, incompatible.

It is clear that our teaching must be flexible enough to help both groups, the ones who look for freedom within the language, who want to experiment, who want to take a chance and the ones who feel that experimentation might lead to the frustration of too many mistakes and even to incomprehensibility, who like the security of being right. **Our teaching must help the careless to be more careful and the careful to be more careless.**

One way of doing this is to stop worrying too much about mistakes! Learning is a mixture of gaining confidence and being adventurous. We should not plan our lessons or write our course-books with the idea of mistakes in the front of our minds. Students should be encouraged to:

gain confidence
be creative
test out new grammar hypotheses
invent vocabulary
practise new structures
and so on.

In any methodology, confidence, fluency and accuracy are needed, but it is always accuracy which is achieved last. The mistakes will come and go, as they always have.

CHAPTER ELEVEN

CORRECTING TASKS

The following are tasks for use by individual teachers or by groups on teacher training or development courses. Each task contains examples of students' work – uncorrected and unmarked. There are two kinds of material:

a. 60 sentences divided into 5 sets

b. 6 full compositions.

Individual sentences

Suggested Tasks:

a. identify the mistake in each sentence

b. using the code which you developed in chapter 7, categorise each mistake

c. rewrite the sentences in correct English

d. using the following code, mark each mistake:

0 points = a slip which is so unimportant as to be hardly worth mentioning

-1 point = a mistake of form, but where comprehension is not impeded

-2 points = shows a fundamental misunderstanding of a particular structure

-3 points = serious mistakes where you do not understand what the student means

(Note: these sentences were given to two groups of non-native speaking teachers of the same nationality and teaching background while attending an in-service teacher training course. They used the marking system of 0 – -3 outlined in the introduction to this task. The marks ranged from the most 'liberal' teacher deducting -17 marks to the most 'reactionary' deducting -57!

The two groups of teachers had had different trainers for their courses. The average marks deducted by one group was -25. The average for the other was -40. In only two of the sentences did the two groups agree. Perhaps these variations tell us something important!)

Set 1

1. She asked me where did I come from.

2. The book was into the bag.

3. The problem was that the door wasn't keyed.

4. He's fond of cooking himself and for me.

5. She was about herself very sensible.

6. Which of the two jokes do you think is best?

7. If I realy want to speak quickly english, I think that the better way is to go into England.

8. If we'd have known about the problem, we would have told you.

9. I am a Spanish girl and I'd like learning English from June to September this year.

10. I would like to know informations about your English course.

11. My favourite book is 'Damien' of Hermann Hesse.

12. Some people and I was looking for the mysterious monster.

13. It is a lively city and expected about the future.

14. Yesterday it really happened something strange.

15. I was affraid because I thought, this guy wants to kill me.

16. How is the earth like?

17. I like very much to read.

18. Many people in my company speaks English.

19. Dear Sir,

    I will go to Cambridge next week, and I'd like to know...

20. For me, is a very attractive place.

Set 2

1. I'm tired. Can we make a break?
2. It happened the same thing to me.
3. We were there on summer.
4. Did you heard what happened this morning?
5. I hope the Government isn't going to higher the taxes.
6. I think the price of books in France is the double.
7. Where's the pen what I left on the desk?
8. Our bags were controlled when we arrived at Gatwick.
9. I think you haven't met her before.
10. I work in export department.

Set 3

1. I give people informations about theatre and such things.
2. I have several brother-in-laws.
3. I have a work in a chemical company.
4. We go out for shopping on Saturday mornings.
5. Where do you eat at lunchtime?
   – I used to have lunch on a coffee bar.
6. Could you do the next one, please?
   – I?
7. I mustn't go out every night. I can stay in and watch TV if I want to.
8. Then after that rings the telephone.
9. When we arrive in the morning, everybody do his own work without talking.
10. We others came later.

Set 4

1. It's been discussing about capital punishment for a few years.
2. She saw two men was leaving Mrs Thompson's house.
3. The second hotel is chipper than the first one.
4. Please reply by litter immediately.
5. My anunt with heir children were stilling also at a strange man were sharing them the cabenit.

6. Our Company chose your Hotel for accommodate the 50 participants of our two-day conference on Monday, 7th December and Tuesday 8th December.

7. Elizabeth went out and knocked her neighbour.

8. Meanwhile the Prince was looking after his animals a big white wolf appeared at the park gate.

9. The children were enthusiast about the day.

10. How is she look like?

Set 5

1. You was remember me of a friend.

2. We do the extrusions plastic.

3. The population was getting more.

4. He seems to be historic teacher.

5. Have you ever been such an experience when you were young?

6. This woman likes to make traditionally pullovers.

7. The TV crew are taking photos for the man.

8. I change my decide.

9. Prices are getting more expensive.

10. When you are bored to wait the train, perhaps you can imagine people around you without trousers.

Compositions and longer passages

Suggested Tasks

a. underline each piece of English which you believe to contain a mistake

b. using the code which you developed in chapter 7, categorise the mistake

c. decide if you think re-writing or reformulation of the passage is i) necessary ii) possible

d. re-write or reformulate the passage if necessary and possible

e. re-read your version and ask yourself if you could re-write any of it into more natural English

f. ignoring the individual mistakes, give each composition a mark out of 10 for communication of content

Correcting Tasks

Composition 1

Dear Sally,

Tank-you for your letter (november 1989!!) your Christmas card and your photos (beautiful). And now Easter is already gone. So I decided to write you, at last.

Life in Cambridge is OK.

We really enjoying our house and our little garden. We bought a rose last sunday called 'golden shower'. Now it is in the garden, and should be claimb along the wall.

We have got a new fence becose the old one was blowed-down from the strong wind 2 months ago.

The last two weeks I worked very hard, from 8.30 in the morning until 7.00 o'clock in the evening, becose we have had a big and urgent order from Japan.

But I'm still very bad pay.

Mike is very busy, too; this evening he is gone to a party. It's half party, half work for him, but it's plenty of drink and music. (I hate partys.)

We are both tired and we need a rest. If we can, we will take a week off in May or June. I'd like to go to Cornowel. And in September we want to go to Crete.

I hope that you are both happy, and with nice jobs, and you Sally OK with your studies.

You are welcome in Cambridge at any time.

I'm looking fourwards to your next letter.

Love,

Francesca

Composition 2

Dear Alberto,

How are you. Thank you letter for me. you will stay here just 2 weeks. but I think too short. because Yokohama is a very big city. and there are a lot of beautiful place.

And I finded a good hotel but I couldn't find park near the hotel but near bud and trin station. so you can simply singtseeing.

Yours

Composition 3

A black train moved from London to Bristol. Two children and their aunt were in the train. After the train moved, a mistery man entered into their compartment and he asked her if I could sit here. He was polite and talkative. Soon, they was chatting very well. Children were glad. Because he started to say an interesting story.

'Once upon a time, a beautiful girl live in a small village. She liked nature so she always went to village of park.

One day she went go to the park again. She walked and sang songs. Then she met a handsome men. He was prince. He was looked good men. While she thought he told her, 'Good morning, what a beautiful day.' In first she was surprised. Then she said 'Good morning, Yes, I think so.' They started to walk together in the park.

But the day wasn't beautiful for sheep and pigs. Because a wolf ran towards them and it attacked to eat them. Prince and girl heart their voice while stand near a small lake. Prince told her to wait here. He was very quick. He used gun and wounded wolf from it's leg. It escaped. Sheep and pigs survived.

In the end of the story, beautiful girl and prince got married and they lived happy until endless.

Mistery man said 'Story finished and I must put in the train.' Children shouted 'DON'T GO, PLEASE, DON'T GO STAY WITH US.'

Composition 4 (in reply to a letter asking for advice)

When I was high-school student same problem. and the first. I asked my good friend; and he said you should be sent letter for her But I couldn't do it. because. I'm too shy. and my friend tought me good advice, he said I suggest you make to her friend and you should about ask her.

Composition 5

Traditional houses

Traditional houses are quite strong, they are cheap to build, they have many disadvantages like the roofs do not last very long, they leak so rats and other animals make their homes there, also they spread disease. The rooms are often very small with many families, they cook in the same area, sometimes small children are sleeping close to the fire, and the toilet may be a long way away. Stairs can be a problem, sometimes too steep, for particularly old people with accidents and broken bones because they fall and hurt themselves, as well as children of course playing on the stairs. But modern flats can be safer and more impersonal, all one on top of the other people can lose the feeling of living in a community being like living in so many little boxes all the same.

Composition 6

As you travel to Hong Kong as a business man, you will not have too much time to sightseeing and you are mostly interested in hotels and shopping.

In Hong Kong the hotels are almost all provided with the best shopping facilities and it will be very easy.

Other shops are easily to reach because of the facilities to move in Hong Kong. Taxis, buses or trams are available at every time of the day and they can bring you to the heart of Hong Kong, Tsim Shei Tsui where shopping is very easy. 'Golden Mile' another district for shopping you will find many jewellery.

Hotels are all surrounded by suberb places to sightsee or to shop. Some Hotels are located near the promenade and the place is very likely for joggers other Hotels are surrounded by ornamental gardens.

I will enclose you some brochures and photos of different hotels so you can make your own choice.

COMMENTARY

Task 2 (page 6)

1. A slip, said on the radio during an interview.

2. A false start. The person started saying: 'Us....' meaning 'in the case of our school' and then continued, thinking, presumably, that school is singular.

3. Used in a lecture, perhaps to stress the hardship.

4. Used in American English.

5. This probably originates from American English, but is increasingly used in (spoken) British English.

6. Traditional grammar books say you should use *fewer*, not *less* with countable nouns, but most modern, descriptive, grammars indicate that both are now 'acceptable'.

7. The use of *There's* (rather than *There are*) with plural nouns is now very common in spoken English.

8. The majority of English people use *best*, even when talking about only two things – most textbooks say you should use *comparatives* with *two* things, and *superlatives* with *three or more*. It is a bit difficult to explain to students that the majority of English people are wrong, so it may not be too wise to correct this point.

9. It is very common to see signs with the apostrophe put in ordinary plurals. Of course, this is a 'mistake' – but before long it may be what everybody does!

10. This is a local form, used in Bristol, meaning 'Where's your purse?' Dialect offers a lot of non-standard English, which while we do not necessarily want to teach it to students, is correctly described as 'non-standard' not 'wrong'.

Task 19 (page 24)

A total of 50 for these sentences would indicate you found them all serious mistakes. A score of 0 indicates you thought there was no mistake at all.

Our scores were as follows:

Numbers 1, 2, 5, 6, 9: 1 point; Number 3: 2 points; Number 4: 2/3 points; Number 7: 1/2 points; Numbers 8, 10: 4 points; **Total 19 points**

Notes:

1. Offends the 'code' but is otherwise comprehensible. In spoken English, it might even be used by native-speakers, especially as part of a list: 'She asked me: where did I come from? was I married? did I like England...'

2. Depending on context, almost certainly comprehensible. (It could just about mean 'The book was put into the bag', but the context would tell you.)

3. 'Keyed' almost certainly stands for 'locked', but it might be misunderstood in certain contexts.

4. Potentially a serious mistake, in the sense that it is ambiguous, but common sense tells us the verb *cook* cannot be reflexive in this case. If the verb were *talking* instead of *cooking*, however, it would be genuinely ambiguous, and therefore more serious. As it stands, it is merely funny.

5. A very small code mistake, but entirely comprehensible.

6. The kind of mistake which teachers loathe, but in fact a sign of learning, and also completely comprehensible.

7. Probably comprehensible (and in spoken English they would be completely so, since they are only spelling mistakes).

8. Two problems: what does *sensible* really mean? and what does *about herself* really mean? This is a classic case where you must go back to the student and find out.

9. This mistake is more complicated than it seems. Obviously, the student has used the present tense rather than the past, but the sentence is clear, because of the time phrase ('last weekend'). There is a case for encouraging students to use these time phrases as much as possible, rather than worry too much about the tense mistake, which is likely to correct itself with time.

10. The problem is '*...expected about the future*'. The context gave us some information – because it was a composition about Barcelona and the forthcoming Olympics. This tells us two things: first, the context is crucial; second, teachers need to take account of local and global factors – see p89.

This gives us a total of between 18 and 20. How does this compare with your score? Do you agree with our discussion?

Task 36 (page 40)

1. The student probably means 'I like going to the cinema very much'. The sentence as it stands seems to imply some technical preference – 'I like film as opposed to video' or '...as opposed to visual arts.' But hardly a significant mistake in most contexts.

2. 'The man ran up to me and pushed me down.' – hardly a covert mistake, as 'ran to me' is usually intended romantically/emotionally. Not a serious mistake, and a good invention on the part of the student. More feedback needed from the teacher.

3. Either '...but I'm well enough now (despite the accident)' or 'but I'm usually healthy (so the accident had little effect)'. We suggest the first, in which case a genuine covert mistake, with more feedback needed.

4. An old favourite. 'Actually' is a false friend i.e. a word which looks like one in other languages, but which means something different. The student may have meant 'At the moment' – you would need to check with the student to find out. This could be a serious mistake – it would depend on the context.

5. The student probably means 'Will you be coming to the school tomorrow?' but as it stands, it seems like a request: 'Please come to the school tomorrow!'

Native-speakers (who are not teachers) could be confused by it:

> Where shall we meet, then?
> Will you come to the school tomorrow?
> I can if you want.
> Yes, but are you coming anyway?
> Um, probably.

This conversation 'negotiates' the meaning, but the student would probably not want to negotiate meaning every time s/he arranges a meeting! For this reason, we would regard it as a reasonably serious mistake, at least at higher levels.

Task 55 (page 63)

1. Correcting the existing sentence would probably change it to:

We succeeded in preventing the flat being burned.

Our suggestion for a full reformulation would be:

We managed to prevent the flat being burned out.

2. **a.** *I thought I was still in my dream.*

   b. *I thought I was still dreaming.*

3. **a.** *My favourite film that I have seen recently is...*

   b. *The best film I have seen recently is....*

4. **a.** *....for a camper.*

   b. *Camping can be a cheap holiday.*

Do you agree with these interpretations? You may find that two or three interpretations are possible, depending on the context.

Task 89 (page 108)
Marking scales based upon rewarding other elements than simple avoidance of mistakes can be reasonably easily drawn up, and need not be subjective. One way might be to decide various criteria for performance, e.g. range of vocabulary, fluency, imagination, achievement of task, and accuracy (more could be added). For each one, the student could be given a score out of 10, where 1=poor and 10=excellent. So a student who was very inaccurate, but did well in the other categories might receive one mark for accuracy, but (say) seven for each of the others, giving a score of 29 out of 50, or 58%. This is not dissimilar to the way some public exams such as Cambridge First Certificate are graded.

In fact, 'impression marks' (where the marker merely records a mark based on his/her impression of the piece of work) need not be subjective, so long as the marker bears in mind the importance of factors other than just accuracy, and can see beyond the simple number of mistakes.